Becoming a Historian

An Informal Guide

Penelope J. Corfield
&
Tim Hitchcock

LONDON
INSTITUTE OF HISTORICAL RESEARCH
UNIVERSITY OF LONDON PRESS

Published by

UNIVERSITY OF LONDON
SCHOOL OF ADVANCED STUDY
INSTITUTE OF HISTORICAL RESEARCH
Senate House, Malet Street, London WC1E 7HU

ISBNs
978-1-914477-15-7 (paperback)
978-1-914477-17-1 (.epub)
978-1-914477-18-8 (.mobi)
978-1-914477-16-4 (.pdf)

DOI
10.14296/202205.9781914477164

Contents

About the authors

PENELOPE J. CORFIELD is Professor Emeritus of History at Royal Holloway, University of London; Visiting Fellow at the University of Newcastle upon Tyne; Member of the Academia Europaea/Academy of Europe; and President of the International Society for Eighteenth-Century Studies (2019–). She has lectured in many countries around the world and welcomes the growth of an 'international sphere' of shared scholarship, intersecting with the already interlocking 'public' and 'private' spheres. Her publications address British social, cultural and urban history in the eighteenth and nineteenth centuries, as well as theories of time and history. Penelope Corfield studied at the universities of Oxford and London (LSE); she has enjoyed supervising many MA and doctoral students; and she continues to learn from family, friends, colleagues, students and correspondents worldwide.

TIM HITCHCOCK is Professor of Digital History at the University of Sussex and, until 2021, was Director of the Sussex Humanities Lab. He has published a dozen books on the histories of poverty, sexuality, gender and crime. With Robert Shoemaker, and others, he has also been responsible for creating a series of web resources, including the *Old Bailey Online*, *London Lives* and *Locating London's Past*, designed to give free public access to the records of the British past and lay the foundation for a 'new history from below'. Following degrees from the University of California at Berkeley and Oxford University, Hitchcock was unemployed for four years before securing a position as a Lecturer in Humanities Computing and Eighteenth-Century Economic History at the Polytechnic of North London in 1989. He moved to the University of Hertfordshire in 1997 and to the University of Sussex in 2013.

CORFIELD and HITCHCOCK are the longest-serving convenors of the British History in the Long Eighteenth Century seminar at University of London's Institute of Historical Research. Between them, they have seventy years (ouch!) of experience watching colleagues and friends navigate an ever-changing professional landscape. This *Guide* is a shared reflection on that experience.

Acknowledgements

With warm thanks to Caroline Barron, Tony Belton, Peter D'Sena, Sonia Hitchcock, Alina McClennan, Doug Munro, Kendra Packham, Stephen Sobey and Jeremy Tee for constructive input; to the stringent anonymous assessors of an early draft text; to Susan Whyman for a perceptive critique of the penultimate version; and to all friends and fellow historians.

Special acknowledgement to the illustrator
The apt illustrations have all been devised by Edwina Hannam, in consultation with the authors, who appreciate her wit, style and visual artistry.

Copyright acknowledgements
Edward Gibbon by Henry Walton © National Portrait Gallery, London (ref: 1443).

Photograph of Gerda Lerner. Gerda Lerner, *c*.1981. Image #S05705 (Uwar01534x). UW-Madison Archives. CC BY 3.0.

Bromide print of E. P. Thompson in National Portrait Gallery NPG P473 © Steve Pyke (1989).

Photograph of Natalie Zemon Davis. Marit Hommedal/SCANPIX (2010). CC BY 2.0.

Photograph of David Olusoga © Ollie Smith at *Epigram* (2018).

Photograph of Olivette Otele © JLK (2020).

Edward Gibbon by Unknown Artist © National Portrait Gallery, London (ref: 3317).

A note on readership

This informal *Guide* is aimed first at apprentice historians writing an MA or MPhil dissertation and, especially, at postgraduates studying for a PhD. These travellers on the educational route to becoming historians cannot plausibly be termed 'beginners', since they must have considerable skills and knowledge to have got this far. Instead, 'apprenticeship' is intended as an affectionate way of signifying that historians work in a craft discipline, in which all are continually learning 'on the job'.

At the same time, the principles and practice of research are relevant to all people who seek to study the past. It is one of the great strengths of history as a subject – and one of its most distinctive characteristics – that significant contributions may come from 'freelancers' working outside the academic world, as well as from specialists within. The route is a shared one. Much of the advice within this *Guide* accordingly applies to all travellers on the road to becoming historians.

By way of clarification, *SIGNPOSTS* are provided within each chapter to indicate whether their contents apply chiefly to an academic trackway or to all comers. Many of the research hurdles as well as the research pleasures are shared ones. Historians, as this *Guide* stresses throughout, are not just found within the academic world. They are potentially everywhere because the past is an open-ended, unstoppable subject that all can study. And a good thing too.

A further note on academic framework

Many detailed references to academic procedures in this book are couched in terms applicable to the British and, to an extent, the English-speaking academic world. Nonetheless, history is a universal subject. And standards in higher education are converging globally. Readers in different educational systems are thus encouraged to focus upon the general points and to translate the practical details into their own different contexts.

Preface

This informal guide to becoming a research historian offers step-by-step advice, as between good friends. Academic history-writing began as a profession of privilege. The old adage that history was 'written by the winners' operated for too long. National archives tended to be records of the world as seen by Western states, while universities began as gatekeepers of class privilege, masculine authority and racial homogeneity. Traditionally, navigating the routes into the academic profession required a good stock of cultural capital, while the abolition of grants and imposition of fees have in effect created a new set of financial hurdles.

But there have been and are slow processes – and sometime more rapid surges – of long-term change. Recruitment into the academic world has broadened. Multiple voices from many different backgrounds are now beginning to share the debates. And the themes that are studied have broadened immensely too. The old focus upon power and state formation has become enriched and challenged by new explorations of gender, identity, ethnic heritage, memory and resistance to power. In sum, the world of history researchers is manifestly not the same as it was in 1920 (100 years ago) or in 1970 (fifty years ago) – or even in 2000 (hardly a generation ago).

Becoming a Historian seeks to provide a practical and down-to-earth guide for all those seeking to circumvent the traditional gatekeepers and to participate in an inclusive community of practice. The world of research at its best is open and sharing. But it can sometimes seem as though its unwritten codes are cliquish and excluding. This *Guide* is dedicated to opening doors. It advises on all the stages of a project, from finding a topic to completion – and onwards after that. It explains the various codes and conventions which operate to underpin an international community of historical researchers.

Furthermore, each journey is a personal adventure. This *Guide* also shares the excitement of research 'highs', when things go well; and offers help for coping with the 'lows', when hours of patient investigations seem to have led nowhere. It also provides real-life case-histories to show how others have travelled these pathways before, while acknowledging that the challenges faced by each new generation of scholars will always be different.

Above all, this *Guide* believes that studying the past is a deeply foundational branch of human knowledge, which simultaneously entails a profound and political engagement with the present. All have a right to participate. The journey takes thought and effort but the processes and debates are endlessly fascinating (and not mysterious). This *Guide* extends the hand of friendship to all comers.

PJC and TH
London
Spring 2022

PART I
Starting, assessing, organizing

1. Joining the through-time community of historians

SIGNPOST: Relevant to all researchers

The community of historians through time, formed of countless experts, whose ranks include:

Top left: Classical China's 'Grand Historian' **Sima Qian** 司馬遷 (*c*.145–*c*.86 BC); top middle: Enlightenment Britain's greatest historian **Edward Gibbon** (1737–94); top right: Trinidadian historian and cultural theorist **C. L. R. James** (1901–89); middle left: French pioneer of multidisciplinary history **Marc Bloch** (1886–1944); centre: Austrian-American trailblazer in women's history **Gerda Lerner** (1920–2013); middle right: guru of 'history from below' and peace activist **E. P. Thompson** (1924–93); bottom left: practitioner of anthropological history **Natalie Zemon Davis** (1928–); bottom middle: leading expert in public (outreach) history **David Olusoga** (1970–); bottom right: historian of slavery and cultural memory **Olivette Otele** (1970–). For further information about these historians, see pp. 15–16

1.1 Defining history

For the purposes of this *Guide*, 'history' refers to the academic and literary discipline of studying the past. The subject has a conscious 'through-time' focus, excavating and debating the encrusted layers of meaning which are attached to earlier events. As a result, history is both a research topic and a process of relating to the past. Generations of practitioners continue to develop the subject and what may appear to be its specialist rituals and trade mysteries. Yet researching history is far from an inexplicable undertaking. This *Guide* offers friendly advice on getting to grips with the subject and on navigating the research process – from finding a subject through to completion and onwards to communicating with the wider world.

It's good to begin with definitions. That is the case especially in the world of historical research, where precision is valued. Naming things accurately is only the 'beginning of wisdom' (as the sage Confucius long ago declared).[1] As a subject, history builds on social memory and shared experiences. Humans live with the past every day. Anyone walking along a street subconsciously acknowledges its impact on the present, as it demarcates the route and delimits alternative options. Equally, people cannot explain a decision without recourse to the story of what led to the moment of choice. Collectively, indeed, humans rely upon a distilled knowledge of things that have gone before.

The formal study of the immensely variegated past overlaps with many other disciplines, including classics, literature, politics, sociology, international affairs and anthropology, to name but a few. Yet history as a subject retains and celebrates its core aims and standards. There are many excellent books addressing its research practices.[2] An associated literature further examines the history of history-writing as a discipline (a specialist field known as historiography).[3] And another group of writings explores

---

[1] R. L. Littlejohn, *Confucianism: an Introduction* (London, 2011).

[2] See L. Jordanova, *History in Practice* (London, 2000); A. Munslow (ed.), *The Routledge Companion to Historical Studies* (London, 2000); J. Tosh with S. Lang, *The Pursuit of History: Aims, Methods and New Directions in the Study of Modern History* (London, 2006); S. Gunn, *History and Cultural Theory* (Harlow, 2006); J. Black and D. M. MacRaild, *Studying History* (Basingstoke, 2007); D. Cannadine, *Making History, Now and Then: Discoveries, Controversies and Explorations* (Basingstoke, 2008); and J. H. Elliott, *History in the Making* (London, 2012).

[3] A. Grafton, *The Footnote: a Curious History* (London, 1997); M. Bentley, *Modern Historiography: an Introduction* (London, 1999); J. Black, *Clio's Battles: Historiography in Practice* (Bloomington, Ind., 2015); D. R. Woolf, *A Concise History of History: Global Historiography from Antiquity to the Present* (Cambridge, 2019).

the theories and philosophy of history (in an emergent field, which is sometimes defined as historiology).[4]

People have written about the past since they first put pen to paper – or stylus to clay – and, even before that, constructed a past through oral tradition. By contrast, the academic discipline of history is little more than two centuries old, albeit building upon earlier roots. Since the eighteenth century in the West, and more particularly since the rise of the university system in early nineteenth-century Germany, history has always been a central subject of academic study, exploring the past in its fullest compass.[5] In so doing, the discipline has evolved a specific relationship to evidence and a known format for producing written arguments, generating a set of conventions which are internationally shared.

This busy world of historical research exists both within and outside formal educational structures. Plenty of historians are 'freelance', writing for love of the subject, and not seeking to hold an academic post. Nonetheless, the values and hierarchies of the university world tend to exert a strong influence, as do the values and hierarchies of the world of publishing. The English Marxist historian E. P. Thompson produced his most famous work, *The Making of the English Working Class* (1963, and still in print), while working in Halifax (Yorkshire) as an extra-mural lecturer for the Workers' Educational Association. For most of his energetic life, he remained a freelancer, with only a relatively short spell as Professor at Warwick University (1965–72).[6] Nonetheless, he acknowledged that, when writing, he became increasingly conscious of the critical gaze of the professionals. The exchange was mutual, as his unorthodox approach and style also influenced Marxist and non-Marxist historians alike.

Influential and sometimes opaque as it can be, however, the academic world should not be viewed as either monolithic or closed. There are multiple

---

[4] J. M. de Bernardo Arès, *Historiology, Research and Didactics: Elaboration and Transmission of Historical Knowledge* (London, 1996); M. Day, *The Philosophy of History: an Introduction* (London, 2008); A. Tucker, *Our Knowledge of the Past: a Philosophy of Historiography* (Cambridge, 2004).

[5] M. Segre, *Higher Education and the Growth of Knowledge: a Historical Outline of Aims and Tensions* (New York, 2015).

[6] E. P. Thompson in 1992 interview with P. J. Corfield, University of London Institute of Historical Research, *Interviews with Historians* (London, 1993). For more on this seminal and much-debated historian, see H. J. Kaye, *The British Marxist Historians: an Introductory Analysis* (Cambridge, 1984); S. H. Rigby, *Marxism and History: a Critical Introduction* (Manchester, 1987); B. D. Palmer, *Objections and Oppositions: the Histories and Politics of E. P. Thompson* (London, 1994); and G. McCann, *Theory and History: the Political Thought of E. P. Thompson* (London, 2019).

gradations of status and hierarchy between universities as well as within them. There are also differences between the various national and cultural traditions around the world. And today, all higher educational systems are facing often contradictory challenges, stemming from the pressures of financial uncertainty, the requirements of public auditing and the civic and political demands for widening access.[7] It is a world at once full of proud certainties from the past and puzzling conundrums in the present.

These factors mean that historians in the making have to negotiate the assumptions, regulations and profound hierarchies of established institutions – but at a time of considerable flux.[8] The research journey is at once personal and professional. It can seem perplexing but should not be mysterious.

1.2 The broad range of historical research

Nothing has happened that cannot, in principle, be studied. Generically, history (the subject) embraces the entire ambit of the past, which is growing every minute. Not only is the evidence expanding but the debates, viewpoints and participants are also constantly multiplying.

In some cases, scholars track backwards to cover the entire lifespan of the cosmos, or simply the evolution of planet Earth. That branch of the discipline is becoming known as big history.[9] It marks a refreshment of scholarly interest in the very long term. The approach, which often combines insights from astronomy, geology and biology, is wonderfully stimulating. It can, however, lead to over-simplification. If there are too many 'big' generalizations, rolling up entire centuries and millennia together, then the details of human history get lost.

At the other end of the spectrum, meanwhile, some scholars focus instead upon micro-histories. Such studies look at specific communities in great depth over a brief span of time. They seek 'To see a World in a Grain of Sand', to borrow William Blake's scintillating dictum.[10] And this

---

[7] See F. Donoghue, *The Last Professors: the Corporate University and the Fate of the Humanities* (New York, 2008); S. Srinivasam, *Liberal Education and Its Discontents: the Crisis in the Indian University* (New Delhi, 2018); J. Frank, N. Gowar and M. Naef, *English Universities in Crisis: Markets without Competition* (Bristol, 2020).

[8] J. M. Banner, *Being a Historian: an Introduction to the Professional World of History* (Cambridge, 2012).

[9] See D. Christian, *Maps of Time: an Introduction to Big History* (London, 2004); updated as D. Christian, *Origin Story: a Big History of Everything* (London, 2018); D. Baker, C. Benjamin and E. Quaedackers (ed.), *The Routledge Companion to Big History* (London, 2019); and thematic discussion in P. J. Corfield, *Time and the Shape of History* (London, 2007).

[10] Opening line of W. Blake, *Auguries of Innocence* (c.1803), in K. Raine, *A Choice of Blake's Verse* (London, 1970), p.31.

approach has been highly effective in uncovering the intricate assumptions and power structures which influence attitudes to class, gender, sexuality, ethnicity, religion and political engagement.[11] But, again, there may be problems if such studies remain too minutely focused without being set in some framing context.

Meanwhile, most historians in practice choose human-scale timespans. They look at groups of centuries rather than millennia; or at decades rather than a single moment. Often, within that, they encompass a great range of issues, and the subject is continually being sub-divided into new fields and sub-fields.[12] And such groups may, especially at first, make space for practitioners to bypass traditional roles and expectations. New themed newsletters, conferences and websites emerge every year, providing a new professional identity to support the new specialism. And these in turn lead to new academic journals, which help to crystallize the field.

Notable examples, among dozens founded in the last forty years, include: the *Historical Journal of Film, Radio and Television* (1981–); the *Animal Studies Journal* (2020–), linking approaches from history and zoology; the interdisciplinary *Journal of Big History* (2017–); and, marking the coming of age of another new field, *Emotions: History, Culture, Society* (2017–).

Stereotypically, the subject was once dismissed as nothing more than telling stories about kings, queens, and battles. Yet such a description was never accurate. The pioneer historians, who formalized the discipline in the eighteenth and nineteenth centuries, looked at the rise and fall of entire cultures. And when rigorous historical methodologies were developed in the nineteenth century, they were designed to allow both national/imperial histories and broad socio-cultural-economic changes to be described and

---

[11] S. G. Magnússon and I. M. Szijártó, *What Is Micro-History? Theory and Practice* (London, 2013). For an urban case-history, see C. Judde de la Rivière, *The Revolt of the Snowballs: Murano Confronts Venice, 1511* (London, Eng. transl. 2018).

[12] Special fields include the following (listed alphabetically): architectural history; art history; biographical history; business history; classical history; comparative history; constitutional history; costume history; cultural history; diplomatic history; economic history, which may include cliometrics (quantitative economic history); environmental history; ethnohistory (studying comparative cultures historically); family history; feminist history; gender history; history of education; history of medicine; history of science; intellectual history and the history of ideas; labour history; legal history; literary history; local history; macro-history; Marxist history; men's history; micro-history; military history; music history; oral history; parliamentary history; political history; prehistory (the eras before the advent of writing); prosopography (group history); public (outreach) history; quantitative history; religious history; social history; subaltern studies (probing post-colonial and post-imperial societies 'from below'); transport history; urban history; women's history; and world/global history.

mapped. Arguably, the subject grew as much from the quest to understand the role of peasants, feudal lords, merchants, industrialists and workers as the activities of monarchs, generals, religious leaders, politicians and philosophers. After all, one of the classic nineteenth-century 'big' thinkers, the polymath Karl Marx, defined his own analysis of the global political economy from primordial times to industrial society (and onwards into the classless future) as a 'theory of history'.[13]

Within this galaxy of approaches and specialisms, scholars today can potentially exercise free choice when deciding their preferred fields of study. They can also change tack in the course of a career, although that option is difficult to implement. One remarkable switch was instanced by Geoffrey Barraclough. He managed an eleven-year stint at Liverpool University as Professor of Medieval History, before in the 1950s changing tack entirely, making a series of institutional and thematic moves, and ending his career at Oxford University as Professor of Modern History, with special expertise in contemporary global affairs.[14]

Today's practitioners, meanwhile, inhabit a rather different world. In some ways, it is intellectually broader. Yet individual scholars often become very specialized, becoming defined in terms of both theme/approach and time/place. As a result, it is easier to become established as an expert on emotion in eighteenth-century Britain than as a historian of emotions through time. Professional historians are, after all, employed by departments or faculties to teach specific subjects; and those subjects in turn have to secure collective approval from colleagues. Many universities (though far from all) make it hard to change the curriculum. Hence, given that academics in post are expected to combine both research and teaching, a structural conservatism acts as a sea-anchor on overly rapid change. So researchers in a tight job market may try to guess at the fields likely to generate demand and adapt accordingly. Yet a degree of flexibility applies as well. New specialisms are constantly emerging, and many individual scholars do manage to evolve their research interests over time. Intellectual rebels and innovators are not always made as welcome on first appearance as they should be. Yet in an ever-developing and broad-based subject, they

---

[13] W. H. Shaw, *Marx's Theory of History* (London, 1978); G. A. Cohen, *Karl Marx's Theory of History: a Defence* (Oxford, 1978, 1987); P. Blackledge, *Reflections on the Marxist Theory of History* (Manchester, 2006).

[14] G. Barraclough (1908–84), *Papal Provisions: Aspects of Church History, Constitutional, Legal and Administrative in the Later Middle Ages* (Oxford, 1935); G. Barraclough, *An Introduction to Contemporary History* (Harmondsworth, 1967); G. Barraclough, *History in a Changing World* (Oxford, 1955); G. Barraclough, *Main Trends in History* (London, 1978).

often provide fresh impetus; and yesterday's rebels can quickly become the gurus of a new specialism.

1.3 The broad church of historical researchers

Defining history broadly means equally that there is a broad church of historical researchers. Their numbers are countless. Plenty are freelance – and all the more welcome for their personal commitment. Mature scholars, in particular, bring welcome expertise and insights from their past experiences in life. All is grist to the historical mills of collective exploration.

But researchers simultaneously inhabit an uneven landscape of authority and engagement. Academic history, while seeking to be welcoming and inclusive, also operates a system of gatekeeping and regulations. Freelance historians working outside the world of academe can, however, choose to adopt the same professional standards – and many do. Meanwhile, current policy in many countries is encouraging universities to look 'outwards'. Established scholars are being encouraged to seek wider audiences in order to demonstrate research 'impact' (see also section 18.4).

It may be noted too that there are additional pressures to expand the amount of interdisciplinary research. Historical research projects already overlap fruitfully with studies in related fields, such as politics, literature, musicology, sociology, art history and so forth. These cross-linkages are a source of renewal for existing research fields, as well as an encouragement to innovation.[15] As a result, interdisciplinary approaches are no longer feared as heresy, but instead applauded as a sign of creativity.

Throughout these changes, there has been a slow – often too slow – evolution in the composition of the professional world of history. For most of the nineteenth and early twentieth centuries, it was a male preserve. Many historians were men of impeccable social status, albeit being joined over time by middle- and working-class recruits. Meanwhile, the first and second waves of feminist activism were also gaining momentum. Outside the academy, women such as Beatrice Webb, Alice Clark and Barbara Hammond helped to expand the subject's range into social history, striking a resonant chord with the reading public.[16] And from the 1960s onwards, female recruits into the universities changed both the characteristic academic

---

[15] See, eg, R. Ghosh (ed.), *The Study of Social History: Recent Trends* (Kolkata, 2013) and W. Steinmetz et al. (ed.), *Writing Political History Today* (Frankfurt, 2013).

[16] For Beatrice Webb, see C. Seymour-Jones, *Beatrice Webb: Woman of Conflict* (London, 1992); for Barbara Hammond, see S. A. Weaver, *The Hammonds: a Marriage in History* (Stanford, Calif., 1997); and for Alice Clark, see M. Berg, 'The first women economic historians', *Economic History Review*, xlv (1992), 308–29.

style and the scope of the discipline, bringing the study of gender, sexuality and patriarchy into the mix. (Though it should not be assumed that all women have to specialize in these fields.)

With such changes, the male photographs that stare from department and faculty walls are gaining more variegated company. But, if gender has been a relative success story in opening the profession, the quest to broaden its ethnic composition has only just begun. The need to incorporate more varied voices from different communities remains absolutely imperative.[17] (Again, with the reminder that scholars can choose their specialisms and do not have to speak solely on issues raised by their personal autobiographies.)

Once, professional historians used to be rather snooty about alternative approaches. For instance, some were gently condescending about genealogists who trace family records and explore a form of micro-history through time. And there were sometimes bitter complaints if the diligent genealogists bagged all the seats in the local archive. Happily, such condescension is less tolerated today. The impulse to recover family history is one of the oldest prompts to understanding the past. It's a motivation which historians should welcome and encourage.[18] Understanding family history helps to give people 'roots'. It also disrupts over-simplified notions of 'identity'. The subject, after all, reveals many instances of population migration, intermarriage and free-wheeling sexual relations, blurring the lines between rival groups. Such themes from the complicated human past may provide a solvent against bigotry and exclusion.

So family history has gained intellectual respectability and come into the fold. Today, however, significant new issues loom. The success of online websites like *Ancestry.co.uk* ('Discover Your Family Story Today!') or *FindMyPast.co.uk* ('Your Ancestors were Amazing!') indicates the scale of public interest. Yet serious questions remain. *Ancestry* has grown from a genealogy tracking tool into an organization which offers DNA-tracing for specified medical conditions. Historians of all stamps watch with some alarm the long-term implications of its sale in August 2020 (for US $4.7 billion) to private equity firm Blackstone Inc.

---

[17] See A. Meier and E. Rudwick, *Black History and the Historical Profession, 1915–80* (Urbana, Ill., 1986); H. L. Smith and M. S. Zook (ed.), *Generations of Women Historians: Within and Beyond the Academy* (Basingstoke, 2018); J. Gallagher and B. Winslow (ed.), *Reshaping Women's History: Voices of Non-Traditional Women Historians* (Urbana, Ill., 2018); H. Chiang et al. (ed.), *Global Encyclopaedia of Lesbian, Gay, Bisexual, Transgender and Queer (LGBTQ) History* (Farmington Hills, Mich., 2019). For contextual trends, see also P. N. Stearns, *Gender in World History* (London, 2015).

[18] For thoughtful introductions, see D. Hey, *Family History and Local History in England* (London, 1987) and D. Hey, *Family Names and Family History* (London, 2000).

Another parallel group of researchers, known as 'antiquarians', used to be treated somewhat disdainfully by professional historians. The noun conjures up an image of a myopic scholar, who collects nuggets of information and then recounts them chronologically. Yet there was often a considerable overlap, especially in the early days. 'Antiquarians' were eighteenth-century scholars who travelled round Britain collecting historic manuscripts and investigating ancient monuments like Stonehenge.[19] So both the Society of Antiquaries of London (founded 1751) and its equivalent in Scotland (founded 1780) added notably to the growth of historical studies.[20]

Over time it was the terminology of 'historian' that became most common, and the professionalizing discipline turned increasingly to the archives, rather than to the physical monuments from the past. (Today, happily, all forms of evidence, material as well as documentary, are called into play.) As a result, old demarcation disputes have faded. Historians form part of a broad church of practitioners, both inside and outside the world of higher education. Anyone from the rawest apprentice to the oldest of old hands may discover something extraordinary and/or formulate a radical new interpretation.

1.4 History students are fellow researchers – not 'customers' who are 'always right'

A recent trend among some politicians and university managers, in the era of fee-paying, has been to urge that students be viewed as 'customers' who have purchased an educational package. Yet changes to the system of university funding, which remain controversial,[21] should not be taken too far in terms of eroding or undermining students' attitudes to learning. After all, they are purchasing an educational programme – *not* a guaranteed degree. Academically, the student-customers are not 'always right'. They do not always get top marks. They are expected to work hard for their degrees.

---

[19] R. Sweet, *Antiquaries: the Discovery of the Past in Eighteenth-Century Britain* (London, 2004); S. Piggott, *William Stukeley: an Eighteenth-Century Antiquary* (London, 1985).

[20] J. Evans, *A History of the Society of Antiquaries* (Oxford, 1956); D. Gaimster et al. (ed.), *Making History: Antiquaries in Britain, 1707–2007* (London, 2007); A. S. Bell (ed.), *The Scottish Antiquarian Tradition … 1780–1980* (Edinburgh, 1981).

[21] For debates, see D. Stager, *Focus on Fees: Alternative Policies for University Tuition Fees* (Toronto, 1989); A. Fazackerley and J. Chant, *More Fees Please? The Future of University Fees for Undergraduate Students* (London, 2010); Spatial Economic Research Centre (SERC – LSE), *Access All Areas? The Impact of Fees and Background on Student Demand for Higher Education in the UK* (London, 2013); S. Riddell et al. (ed.), *Higher Education Funding and Access in International Perspective* (London, 2018).

And, in return, they expect high-quality courses and individually tailored feedback for their efforts.

Tutors of doctoral students for their part offer a mixture of personal encouragement and intellectual criticism. They give credit for the technical presentation and historical content of all works submitted (draft chapters, reports and so forth), whether they (the tutors) personally agree with the arguments or otherwise. It is a professional but also a deeply personal process. At heart, the exchanges between tutors and research students constitute a dialogue between two thinking individuals, which generates camaraderie of mutual effort.

Money can't buy the experience of historical understanding. Instead, researchers gain expertise by well-sustained effort, supported by apt encouragement and criticism from their tutors and often from fellow students as well. (See chapter 12 on troubleshooting.)

There is a further critical dimension to the research students' commitment which also needs frank acknowledgement. They have no guarantee of certainty of outcome. The great expansion of access to academic life since the 1960s has allowed many more people access to advanced research – and to the sheer joy and passion it can generate. Yet there is an attendant risk of raising expectations which cannot be guaranteed, particularly in terms of jobs at the end of the research journey. In 1969, the number of history doctorates awarded in the UK was no more than twenty, although there was probably some under-recording in an era of much more casual record-keeping. Since then, there has been a veritable explosion of activity. In 2015 the comparable number was 545.[22] Successful research historians with a doctorate are therefore entering a world of competition and precariousness.

Most will in fact get employment in a range of challenging and exciting fields. The extent of unemployment among research historians is low. However, it is worth stressing from the start that there is no guarantee of any specific type of job. And, in particular, there is absolutely no guarantee of an academic job as a university lecturer. Vacancies appear in a sporadic fashion. Sometimes there are years when many junior posts are advertised; but in other years there may be none. As a result, those hoping to join the ranks of academe may spend years in part-time or temporary appointments, even while they compile an impressive portfolio of publications and outreach experience in hopes of opportunities yet to come. (See more in chapters 18 and 19.)

---

[22] Data for 2015 from British Library Ethos system; compared with earlier evidence in University of London's Institute of Historical Research, *List of Theses Completed* (1969).

Happily, the world of research history is changing, and becoming considerably more inclusive, even when navigating the world of higher education remains difficult. Research students are thus fellow scholars in a joint endeavour. They are not 'customers'. But they are not learners on a guaranteed pathway either. They are highly likely to gain their doctorates, as drop-out and failure rates have been sharply cut in recent years by professional supervision and training. Nevertheless, researchers also live in a wider world that combines both uncertainty and opportunity. The broader result is that, while access to research qualifications is regulated by the universities, the resultant research community stretches well beyond the traditional confines of academe.

1.5 Upholding research standards

All historians rely upon getting critical assessments of their work. Much of the one-to-one interchange between research students and supervisors is a form of peer review. Other responses come in the form of seminar discussions, book reviews, personal exchanges and anonymous assessments, written for publishers and academic journals. At its best, the process of being criticized and edited is productive and enlightening. It's true that the experience can at times be a challenge to the ego. Yet it's absolutely invaluable. As a result, all serious researchers, from the most experienced to the newest apprentice, submit to peer review to weed out inadvertent blunders, omissions, inconsistencies and lack of clarity. Indeed, the verdict may be a thumbs down, as well as the reverse.

After all, historical research is not all of equal value. Some studies are done casually, sloppily, badly, misleadingly and even fraudulently. The 'open house' of research does not mean that there are no standards. One very basic requirement is to document the evidence. Works of fiction do not need factual proof. Valid historical studies do. The level of detail varies with the style of presentation and the intended audience. A popular piece of history-writing often provides suggestions for 'further reading'; a slightly more academic publication or 'trade book', intended for wide distribution, usually manages with brief endnotes, squirreled at the back in order not to break readers' concentration; and a fully academic monograph tends to have footnotes on each page, so that conscientious readers can check the sources as they read. In all cases, the need to document the supporting evidence is a staple of scholarly presentation.

Works of history thus indicate visually on every page that they are serious productions. Footnotes or endnotes invite readers to give their trust. But equally, it is up to authors to decide how they wish to present their work. To take one example, the absorbing study, entitled *Secondhand Time: the*

Last of the Soviets by Svetlana Alexievich, has justly won a Nobel Prize for Literature.[23] She charts the emotional costs of living through turbulent times, citing graphic reflections from oral history interviews with unknown Russians, who recounted their experiences under the rule of the Soviets and their successors. However, no sources are cited. Their authenticity has to be taken on trust. In other words, Alexievich's wonderful literary evocation is not a substantiated historical study.[24] (For more on the boundaries between fiction and history, and on the need to cultivate a good, accessible writing style, see chapter 7.)

Interestingly, however, many historians these days do study emotions and feelings, along with everything else (as already noted).[25] And Alexievich's evidence, which crucially relates to major themes in recent Russian history, would make a huge contribution to the subject. Historians would therefore welcome a deposit of her interview transcripts in an oral history archive. Such material is now accepted as a great resource (as noted below). Obviously, it's for authors to decide how they want to write. But readers are equally entitled to judge the results. How much or little did the author invent? Literary works (like films) often play a great role in triggering the historical imagination.[26] They venture beyond and 'behind' the documented sources. As a result, they can bridge sympathetically between popular culture and specialist studies. However, historical romances have free licence to invent.

Historians, on the other hand, are expected to conform to a rigorous system of validation, citing all their sources and methods, as they attempt the difficult task of differentiating between fact and fiction.

1.6 Summary: joining in

Studying the past is an awkward exercise – a balancing act between controlled imagination, the power of logical argument and the presence of evidence on the page. It generates a fine tension between enthusiasm and scepticism.

Historians simultaneously operate within a global community of practice. Individual researchers are invited to join a long-standing and massive human

[23] S. Alexievich, *Secondhand Time: the Last of the Soviets* (Moscow, 2013; in Engl. transl. by B. Shayevich, New York, 2016).

[24] Alexievich, *Secondhand Time*, p. 7.

[25] See J. Plamper, *The History of Emotions: an Introduction*, transl. K. Tribe (Oxford, 2015); B. H. Rosenwein and R. Cristiani, *What Is the History of Emotions?* (London, 2018); R. Boddice, *The History of Emotions* (Manchester, 2018); and a fine exemplar in S. Holloway, *The Game of Love in Georgian England: Courtship, Emotions and Material Culture* (Oxford, 2019).

[26] K. Mitchell and N. Parsons (ed.), *Reading Historical Fiction: the Revenant and Remembered Past* (Basingstoke, 2013).

endeavour that spans generations. They are part of not just a 'dialogue' between a specific period in the past and the present day, but a positive 'plurilogue', whereby today's researchers not only explore the past but also mentally commune with all who have studied the same period across the generations. It's a subject based upon communal discussions, which is why researchers are also encouraged to teach.[27] Anyone ready to enter the debates and critique the sources can join.

Conceptually, history is a universal subject, open to all – even if in practice it can often feel exclusionary and privileged. Understanding its researchers as participating in a shared community, putting their shoulders to a common wheel, makes a fine start.

Further information on historians depicted at head of chapter:

For **Sima Qian** 司馬遷 (*c*.145–*c*.86 BC), see B. Watson, *Ssu-Ma Ch'ien: Grand Historian of China* (New York, 1958).

For **Edward Gibbon** (1737–94), see C. Roberts, *Edward Gibbon and the Shape of History* (Oxford, 2014).

For **C. L. R. James** (1901–89), see R. Douglas, *Making the Black Jacobins: C.L.R. James and the Drama of History* (Durham, N.C., 2019).

For **Marc Bloch** (1886–1944), see F. Hulak, *Sociétés et mentalités: la science historique de Marc Bloch* (Paris, 2012) and M. Bloch, *The Historian's Craft*, transl. by P. Putnam (Manchester, 1954, 1967).

For **Gerda Lerner** (1920–2013), see her publications *The Creation of Patriarchy* (New York, 1986) and *Fireweed: A Political Autobiography* (Philadelphia, Pa., 2003).

For **E. P. Thompson** (1924–93), see C. Efstathiou, *E.P. Thompson: A Twentieth-Century Romantic* (London, 2015) and H. J. Kaye and K. McClelland (ed.), *E.P. Thompson: Critical Perspectives* (Oxford, 1990).

For **Natalie Zemon Davis** (1928–), see G. Murdock and others (ed.), *Ritual and Violence: Natalie Zemon Davis and Early Modern France* (Oxford, 2012).

---

[27] For public presentation, see ch. 13. And for teaching guides, see J. Cannon, *Teaching History at University* (London, 1984); T. M. Kelly, *Teaching History in the Digital Age* (Ann Arbor, Mich., 2013); R. B. Simon et al. (ed.), *Teaching Big History* (Oakland, Calif., 2015); A. Flint and S. Jack, *Approaches to Learning and Teaching History: a Toolkit for International Teachers* (Cambridge, 2018); W. Caferro, *Teaching History* (London, 2019).

For **David Olusoga** (1970–) on the global meetings of cultures, see his *Black and British: A Forgotten History* (London, 2016) and his *First Contact: Cult of Progress* (London, 2018).

For **Olivette Otele** (1970–), see her *African Europeans: An Untold History* (London, 2020), and as editor (with others), *Post-Conflict Memorialisations: Missing Memorials, Absent Bodies* (London, 2021).

2. Launching the research project

SIGNPOST: The first two sections are revelant to all researchers; the third and fourth specifically to those seeking a doctoral supervisor.

Kindling the research flame.

2.1 *Finding the topic*

First, it's essential for all researchers to find a stimulating research topic, with a theme or question which genuinely interests them, which they believe to be important, and for which they have suitable aptitudes and interests.[1]

Hence those who can't do advanced maths should not choose quantitative economic history; those who can't read French and have no time to learn should not specialize in French history; and so forth. Some institutions will help early career researchers to improve recondite skills (such as medieval Latin for historians) or to learn a new one from scratch. Such opportunities help to improve access to sub-fields with special requirements. Indeed, all chances of learning new skills are to be welcomed. Sometimes people surprise themselves by overcoming old inhibitions (or dismissive remarks from others) to blossom in unexpected ways. However, basic interests and aptitudes should still be borne in mind. Research projects can also take many literary forms. Taking these points into account, someone seeking to write empathetic narratives about individual experiences should not sign up for a mathematically complex study in econometric history – or vice versa.

Because finding the right research topic is so crucial, it's wise to take time and to consult over options. Many academics, archivists, librarians and museum curators are happy to discuss possibilities and make suggestions. And researchers should consult their own central inclinations, thinking hard about which area, or period, or type of history they find most fascinating. People are sometimes inspired by personal experience, or by a great teacher, or by an inspiring book. Or simply by a great research question.

The chosen topic should then have some significance that makes it worth pursuing throughout a long project. It could address an issue of contemporary concern. Or a controversy within the historical literature. Or a new theme which the researcher plans to highlight. Yet it is simultaneously essential to bear in mind that the precise topic is likely to be subtly – and sometimes not so subtly – refined and adapted in the course of research. It is a relatively common experience to begin grappling with the original sources, only to discover that unexpected possibilities are revealed while expected options falter. Knowledge creation thus proceeds in dialogue with the historical evidence.

---

[1] See A. Brundage, *Going to the Sources: a Guide to Historical Research and Writing* (Hoboken, N.J., 2018); D. Silverman, *Doing Qualitative Research: a Practical Handbook* (London, 2009); J. Felton et al., *The Professional Doctorate: a Practical Guide* (Basingstoke, 2013); and a classic account by M. Bloch, *The Historian's Craft*, transl. P. Putnam (Manchester, 1954, 1967).

One practical point to consider is the location of the key archives or source collections for any given topic. A project that requires extensive travel to distant locations will be hard to complete without both financial support and extended periods of dedicated time. Digitization has made many sources newly accessible en masse. Yet it has also raised the allure and prestige of distant archives.[2]

In some cases, researchers claim that their research topic found them, as it were. They may wish to explore themes in their own family or community history which have been ignored or under-studied in traditional studies, yet are crying out for attention. Or there may be issues which the researcher considers to have been treated with bias and which await a seasoned reconsideration.

Or they may simply have made a lucky find. Sometimes researchers do stumble across previously unknown sources relating to an important theme. It's called research 'serendipity' (a wonderful stroke of luck – an abstraction coined by Horace Walpole in 1754, borrowing from an old Persian tale of the fortunate princes of Serendip). Nevertheless, self-knowledge still applies. Potential researchers who have found marvellous new sources should consider whether their systematic study falls within their own capacities. If yes, then all well and good. If not, then it's best to alert another researcher or an appropriate archive to the marvellous new sources and to find another great topic instead.

Long-term projects often develop in unexpected ways. And the eventual answers may not be those anticipated at the start. But that's the whole point of research. Starting is not the same as arriving. One project that mushroomed was commenced in the 1980s by Edmund Green, then a postgraduate in London, now a freelance scholar and Liverpool University Research Fellow. He wanted to disprove the late E. P. Thompson's analysis of working-class radicalism in late eighteenth-century Westminster.[3] Green's work gradually extended into a lifetime's study, covering the entire electoral history of metropolitan London from 1700 to 1850. On the way, as it happens, Thompson's analysis of working-class radicalism was confirmed. Yet the project moved well beyond its initial target, illuminating an active electoral culture, operating at parliamentary, municipal and ward levels. Moreover, Green discovered evidence for hundreds of local elections,

[2] L. Putnam, 'The transnational and the text-searchable: digitized sources and the shadows they cast', *American Historical Review*, cxxi (2016), 377–402.
[3] The debated proposition was the propensity of working-class voters in the 1790s to vote for radical candidates who supported parliamentary reform: see E. P. Thompson, *The Making of the English Working Class* (London, 1963; 1968 edn), pp. 491–514.

hitherto unknown to historians.[4] His project is a great example of how a finite question can open many research doors.

An alternative example shows how an unexpected documentary find has raised major political as well as historical issues for debate. While researching his MA thesis, Nick Draper encountered in Britain's National Archives full accounts of the recorded 'reparations' paid to slave owners after the abolition of slavery in 1833.[5] Eventually, he and other colleagues greatly expanded the project. They established the 'Legacies of British Slave-Ownership' database.[6] That authoritative resource now shows how profits from the Caribbean plantations, with their enslaved workforces, percolated through the British economy – and into the household accounts of many a stately country mansion. The evidence is also directly relevant to current arguments about 'reparations' or equivalent acknowledgement to the descendants of the great historical injustice of enslavement – a big outcome from one documentary find.

Once a research project has been launched and funded, it's important for both student and university that the project be completed. For that reason, many institutions give careful warnings at the start. Big research projects are not for everyone. They take time. They require mental effort. They can be mentally isolating (though tutors try to prevent that from happening). And they can prove depressing if things don't always go well. It's as well to confront such realities at the very start. Then those who decide to continue have had fair warning. And, hearteningly, many apprentice researchers declare that they do have the motivation to overcome all obstacles. That's the best response. It marks the kindling of the burning desire – and the motivation to keep going throughout the long haul. And – just to stress again – finishing a big project takes years of effort. Many plans are short-term things: a matter of weeks or months. This one takes years.

Ultimately, researchers themselves have to supply the burning desire to under-take the task. Supervisors can and do exhort, encourage and offer training.[7]

[4] E. M. Green, P. J. Corfield and C. Harvey, *Elections in Metropolitan London, 1700–1850, Vol. I: Arguments and Evidence*; *Vol. II: Metropolitan Polls* (Bristol, 2013); Eighteenth-Century Political Participation and Electoral Culture project (dir. M. Grenby et al.) at the University of Newcastle upon Tyne.

[5] <https://web.archive.org/web/20220209083404/https://www.ucl.ac.uk/lbs/project/draperinterview> [accessed 9 Feb. 2022].

[6] <https://www.ucl.ac.uk/lbs/project/details> [accessed 29 April 2021].

[7] J. McMillan, *Using Students' Assessment Mistakes and Learning Deficits to Enhance Motivation and Learning* (London, 2016); R. J. Wlodkowski, *Enhancing Adult Motivation to Learn: a Comprehensive Guide for Teaching All Adults* (San Francisco, Calif., 2017).

Yet the main motivation has to come from within.[8] Potential researchers sometimes then ask: how burning should the burning desire be? Maybe not a total conflagration from the very start. Yet it should be a genuine self-tended spark that can gain strength as things proceed. Whatever the chosen theme, there should be one who believes in its significance throughout: that is, the person tending the flame.

2.2 Finding the sources

BUT! Before finally deciding, the second requirement is that there must be sufficient and relevant original sources accessibly in existence or (in some statistical subjects) capable of being compiled/calculated, which will enable the study to be completed within a finite period of time.

Of course, not all forms of historical writing have to be based upon original sources. Textbooks, overview essays, book reviews – these are all valuable contributions in their different ways. Yet original research needs original sources. In other words, historians seek evidence which has not yet been studied in depth or which has been viewed, perhaps cursorily, some time ago and is ripe for reconsideration.

By the way, there is no limit to the range of materials that count as historical sources. Everything and anything from the past can be studied systematically. Historians don't have to confine themselves to documents in archives. Instead, the golden rule is to cast the net widely. There are amazing quantities of untapped and under-used original sources out there, waiting to be found in archives, libraries, museums, art galleries, monumental buildings and so forth. 'Going fishing' will find a number of duds but also great treasures.

A research topic works best with a conjunction of good research questions and a good stock of relevant sources. Both are needed. Furthermore, for those wishing to proceed to a doctorate, the sources should be relatively accessible and sufficiently substantial and cohesive to make writing a big study feasible in a finite number of years. It's also helpful to think ahead about possible career pathways. Giving projects a focused comparative dimension may improve a researcher's portfolio in the eyes of future employers. (Supervisors' advice can be especially helpful here.) By contrast, at post-doctoral level, it's fine to collect scattered sources on difficult topics, taking twenty years to amass fragments of material. It adds zest to research to have some apparently 'impossible' subjects in mind. And sometimes such scattergun projects bear magnificent fruit.

---

[8] F. Coombes, *Successful Self-Motivation* (London, 2011); A. Tannock, *The Self-Motivation Workbook* (London, 2015); and a huge literature on self-improvement.

Yet the postgraduate researcher needs to be more practical (funding and time are not limitless) and more immediately focused. Learning how to make and sustain a thesis is a finite task. Again, it's good to take time and to ask many experts for advice. Matching topics and sources together is a necessary first stage in what may become a major quest. As a result, it's a time of exploration, when the research kindling is being assembled, for eventual igniting into fire.

2.3 Finding a supervisor

Third, then, both topic and relevant sources need to be matched with an inspiring, pro-active supervisor. Such a mentor need not be an absolute world expert on precisely the chosen subject. Indeed, there can be problems if the specialist research fields are too closely overlapping. On the other hand, it's helpful if the supervisor has a good general understanding of the relevant field.

Direct face-to-face discussion is much the best way to find such a mentor. And it's quite acceptable to talk to more than one person before deciding. A four-year research partnership is a big undertaking. It's worth taking time to decide who can best provide help and personal inspiration. Email enquiries can also be used as a preliminary filter. If a potential supervisor's first response is a claim to be too busy, too grand or too lacking in interest to meet a new researcher, then the relationship is not likely to thrive.

Some institutions are happy for supervisors and prospective PhD students to agree that matter between themselves – after which the student of course has to make a formal application and gain acceptance. But some other places expect candidates to apply 'blind'. In that case, researchers simply submit an application to one or more places where they would like to enrol.

Only when accepted are they allocated to a PhD supervisor by the department or faculty. In such cases, it's important to make a fairly quick assessment as the relationship develops. The first term or semester should be taken as a testing period. If things are not going well at the end of that trial time, then the postgraduate organizer should be informed, in as calm and polite a manner as possible. Incompatible matches can go sour – and the longer they are left unchanged, the more problems may emerge. It can be difficult to raise such issues with a supervisor who is viewed as an authority figure; but it is much better for everyone to get things right from the start.

A different set of considerations need to be kept in mind when making applications: namely, the need to find research funding. The situation here can be fast-changing. So the onus is upon the researcher to hunt around, using ingenuity and enterprise. The annual *Grants Register* provides an excellent starting-point.[9] The Institute of Historical Research also produces an invaluable list of potential sources of funding.[10] Important institutional sources include Britain's research councils (the Arts and Humanities Funding Council (AHRC); the Economic and Social Research Council (ESRC)).[11] Funding for doctoral study from the councils is now organized through regional consortia of universities. Many institutions also fund degrees on their own behalf, as do local and national educational charities, and specialist research foundations such as the Wellcome Trust for health/medical history.[12]

Furthermore, large-scale externally funded projects can often include support for doctoral students as part of a bigger programme. These initiatives then provide a perfect research environment by creating a ready-made community of people with shared scholarly interests. Yet it is important that researchers consult their own aptitudes and motivation before applying. Working on someone else's project might deliver an income, but success in the role depends upon being able to contribute genuine energy and enthusiasm.

Styles of supervision have changed mightily over the years. Old-style supervisors were not always effective. Now, however, a pro-active partnership is the ideal, and systems for monitoring supervision are much more robust. It's perfectly okay to ask potential supervisors about their supervisory strategies, and what results they have had with previous supervisions. If they look blank and can't reply, then the new researcher should beware. At the same time, allowances should be made for young academics who are new supervisors. They are often very keen and inspiring, learning the ropes alongside their research students. And all will be helped by the departmental or faculty code of practice, which now advises on standard procedures.

2.4 Seeking positive support, not empty prestige

When making the choice of institution or supervisor, there may also be socio-psychological pressures, perhaps from friends and family, to find the

---

[9] A crucial source is Palgrave Macmillan's annual publication, *The Grants Register 2019: the Complete Guide to Postgraduate Funding Worldwide* (2019), available online: <https://www.palgrave.com/gp/book/9781349958092> [accessed 29 April 2021].

[10] <https://web.archive.org/web/20190403052731/https://www.history.ac.uk/history-online/grants> [accessed 9 Feb. 2022].

[11] <https://web.archive.org/web/20220318041734/https://www.ukri.org/opportunity/> [accessed 18 March 2022].

[12] <https://web.archive.org/web/20220117201811/https://wellcome.org/grant-funding/schemes/four-year-phd-programmes> [accessed 17 Jan. 2022].

most outwardly prestigious person as a supervisor, or the most traditionally prestigious institution as an academic home. Such moves are defended as being 'realistic': planning for one's future career by associating with 'the best'. But such thinking can lead to later problems. Sometimes prestigious academics in established posts are too busy. Or sometimes the prestigious institution is too complacent about its appeal and leaves students to sink or swim in isolation. Hence applicants who go for 'prestige' without other supporting benefits – a caring supervisor who has time to supervise – will find that they are left with nothing other than fool's gold.

Needless to say, the world of research is not in practice a perfect meritocracy. That state of affairs obtains partly because opinions differ as to how to identify the best candidates for historical research, and partly because, sad to relate, some old-style patrons still like to collect obedient 'followers'. It is also true that institutions of higher education have still not managed to escape entirely all racist, sexist and classist attitudes which prevail (and are contested) within the wider society.

Nonetheless, a belief in scholarly merit does underpin the world of research – and provides its lifeblood. In recent years, well-meaning attempts have been made to regularize and make accountable systems of appointment and selection. Embryonic historians are not best identified by the schools they attended; or by the families from which they come; or by their social, religious or ethnic backgrounds more generally. They are identified by their aptitudes and enthusiasm.

It equally follows that research success will not come simply from having a famous supervisor or from belonging to a famous research institution. In the spirit of meritocracy, therefore, a new apprentice needs to find the best supervisor for the research project in hand, who can provide a mix of both organizational support and intellectual engagement.

2.5 Summary: 'owning' the project

To recap: researchers need interesting and challenging big themes or research questions to investigate, which they believe are important, whether politically, culturally or academically. They need good, accessible and relevant sources. And they need competent and intellectually challenging supervisors. Working together is positively bonding. The ideal is thus to generate a shared camaraderie, which helps everyone through a long project. Finally, researchers should individually 'own' their chosen history projects, so that they can explain them clearly to the wider world. And, best of all, do so with genuine zest.

3. Shared monitoring of the timetable

SIGNPOST: Relevant specifically to those studying for a higher degree – and to their supervisors. But the general advice on finding ways to set and manage a timetable is relevant to all researchers.

Fanning the research flames, from first spark to maximum intellectual firepower.

3.1 Framing the timetable

Once the researcher and supervisor are paired, it is essential for both parties to agree in framing and monitoring the timetable. Embarking on a big project entails settling in for a long slog. It usually takes three to four years to research, write and present to publishable standard an original study of 80,000–100,000 words; to make, in the words of most university regulations, 'an original contribution to knowledge'. That's a big personal investment in time and effort, especially given that there will be moments of doubt, illness and sundry life crises, as well as moments of euphoria. (By the way, there are a small number of people with funds and years to spare who do truly want a lifetime project. That objective may be fine in a few special cases, but they can't expect a lifetime supervisor.)

The standard for a four-year PhD, amounting to at least 80,000 and no more than 100,000 words in some eight to ten chapters, will therefore include something like the following (to be adapted according to length of thesis, nature of the research and time available):

YEAR 1: Write: review of historiography; review of sources; review of methodology; at least one research chapter (preferably two)

YEAR 2: Pass progression interview; and write three to four research chapters

YEAR 3: Give a paper to a research seminar; write three to four research chapters

YEAR 4: Revise all chapters; write an Introduction and Conclusion, incorporating a revised version of the literature review plus source critique; compile booklist of works consulted (bibliography); submit thesis for examination; and wait anxiously for the oral examination (viva)

Working to an agreed timetable helps to even out the mood swings that accompany the long slog. There will be moments of happy absorption, but also periods of boredom, isolation, exasperation, wrong turns and discouragement that may even risk burn-out. That last fate used to be far too common in the days before close supervision and tight deadlines. Researchers left completely to their own devices often got lost – many imagining that the degree required an impossible standard of perfection. As a result, numerous excellent projects were not completed, to the researchers' own chagrin and dismay.

Nowadays, things are different, and university regulations explicitly stipulate that the final thesis should be judged against what can reasonably be expected at the end of three to four years' work, in the case of a PhD. So it really helps to be explicit about expectations and time management from the start. The supervisor's aim is to help the postgraduate finish a big project not only well – that goes without saying – but also within a specified time.[1]

Time-keeping matters for both practical and intellectual reasons. People don't have unlimited years and funds to produce their great work. And grant-funding bodies insist upon finite timetables. Furthermore, planning and revising a big work, under supervision, teaches the invaluable discipline of mental time management. No-one can hold the totality of 100,000

---

[1] See G. Wisker, *The Good Supervisor: Supervising Postgraduate and Undergraduate Research for Doctoral Theses and Dissertations* (Basingstoke, 2012); J. Wellington et al. (ed.), *Succeeding with Your Doctorate* (London, 2005); and on time management, R. Krznanic, *Carpe Diem Regained: the Vanishing Art of Seizing the Day* (London, 2017).

words of argument and evidence in the proverbial mind's eye. Breaking a large project down into shorter sections helps. Often, the final argument will only begin to emerge through the process of writing several short sections. And sensible intermediate due dates, within an agreed framework, are mentally and organizationally helpful: when all's said and done, *there's nothing like a real deadline.*

Moreover, not only does producing a research thesis take a long time, but the finicky finishing processes, which involve checking and checking again, down to every last dot and comma, can also drive many people to distraction. The end so often seems near. Yet it often turns out not to be quite as near as hoped.

In fact, the very last stages are highly educational (see chapter 16). Returning to a chapter written perhaps two years earlier is a revelation, and usually reflects just how much progress has been made. Each near-to-final iteration produces a visible improvement, and sometimes a major leap forward. It takes a lot of effort and well-directed perseverance to get there, and even with hard work, no project will ever be absolutely perfect. But the process of getting it 'good enough' is part of the discipline. The challenges along the way are perfectly normal – and there are well-established ways of coping.

3.2 Shared monitoring of the state of play

Another framework rule thus follows logically. Researchers should report regularly to supervisors, who should help to ensure that the scale of the project matches the allotted time for completion. This point is particularly crucial. The research process will generate new leads, new approaches, new possibilities. Excellent. But the 'exploding galaxy' needs to be kept under control. Some possibilities may have to be 'parked' for post-doctoral research. Here the supervisor's experience is useful in keeping the project under control.

Checking the timetable therefore requires regular consultation between supervisors and researchers, on at least a quarterly basis. Some institutions require a precise schedule of meetings – often monthly – with frequent reports, and specified levels of engagement to be achieved. As things progress, meetings and checks should become more frequent. At all points, discussions need to be based on frank disclosure. It's fatally easy to kid oneself – and others. The worst thing is to claim airily: 'Oh, it's nearly finished'. Sometimes incautious listeners are convinced. But such vague assurances should be distrusted.

Hence, for any big project, it's imperative to take stock realistically and, as needed, reconfigure either the timetable or the overall plan, or both.

There's no discredit in making changes. In fact, it's a common experience, depending upon the availability and usefulness of the sources. Checking, reassessing, rethinking and, if need be, revising the plan is an integral part of creativity. It's the equivalent of tending the fire; fanning the flames while preventing the blaze from either burning out or spreading out of control. It is also essential to let supervisors check output regularly. It is part of their job to help in sifting gold from the dross, and to enable researchers to produce the very best they can.

These days, indeed, most institutions of higher education encourage regular planning. And they provide a departmental or faculty review process, known as the progression or 'upgrade' viva, or oral interview. It's essential to make that into a serious hurdle. It is usually held at the end of the first year, or in the first term of the second year. And it takes the form of an interview, with an experienced set of colleagues, to whom the researcher presents the thesis plan and a specified number of chapters (often the historiographical review and one research chapter). The format mimics that of the completion viva at the end of the degree, providing good advance practice.

If things are going well, then surmounting the progression viva will fuel the research fires positively. But, if there really are serious problems, then it's best to acknowledge those problems and seek a solution. In some (rare) cases, researchers withdraw entirely and move on to something else. That outcome is tough. But it's better for all concerned to realize before too much time and effort has been expended. Learning to weld ambitious dreams with practical realism is not just a good business or research skill – it's a tool for life.

3.3 Negotiating the deadlines

To make the system work effectively, the researcher should always be working to an interim deadline, agreed with the supervisor. Such internal targets are all-important. Researchers should never be left drifting without knowing what they are doing next. The big project is accordingly sub-divided into standard stages, each being undertaken to a specific deadline. At each review point, the researcher will normally submit a written report or draft chapter, ideally completed to a high standard of technical presentation, complete with finished footnotes. But even if the work is not fully polished, it is important to get something on paper, and to meet intermediate deadlines. These early drafts will all contribute to the finished thesis. They are therefore 'banked' as components of the final text, for further polishing/amending at the very end.

Setting these interim deadlines is a matter for negotiation between supervisors and researchers. The supervisor should ensure that the targets are not unrealistic. But it is then the researcher's prime responsibility to 'own' the timetable. If the deadline can be met, then all's well. But if it proves unrealistic in practice (as frequently happens), then the researcher should take the initiative and contact the supervisor to negotiate an extension. It should not be a melodrama. Simply a notification that another week, or fortnight, or some other timespan is required. Supervisors will generally agree without question. The point is that researchers should never be allowed just to crash through a deadline without anyone noticing. That way there follows, after the initial illusion of relief on the part of the researcher, a deep demoralization.

In sum, purposeful research needs sensible deadlines, which are sufficiently flexible to take account of the vagaries of research. Finding new material and developing new ideas are big, challenging tasks which don't necessarily run to strict timetables. But that undeniable fact does not mean that projects should drop off the radar. It just means that timetables and deadlines need adjustment.

By the way, it also helps if all postgraduate researchers are encouraged to keep closely in touch with their peer group. Facilitating wider contacts, within and outside the immediate institution, is a key task for supervisors, especially at the start. Averting isolation makes for happier and more productive researchers. Consulting with others, after formal seminars or after any informal gatherings, is a vital mechanism for getting and giving mutual support. (See too chapter 8 on using social media.)

Academic supervisors have many other tasks. They may well ask constantly how things are going. But they are not expected to give day-by-day direction. Sometimes apprentice historians expect too much top-down management and become disappointed when that's not on offer. At other times, by contrast, researchers may be too obstinately independent, failing to benefit from the supervisors' multifarious contributions, which range from monitoring progress to reading drafts, advising on seminar presentations and assisting with career development. The aim is a scholarly partnership. So, if there are times, between scheduled meetings, when further discussion is needed, it's for the researchers to take the lead, contacting the supervisors as required. That's good and normal. Cooperation, consultation and mutual debate are the keystones.

3.4 *Writing constantly*

Thus, researching and writing are the twin legs which enable history projects to advance. No supervised researcher should be without a target deadline for a forthcoming report, interim paper or draft chapter. Some supervisors go so far as to demand the production of a specific number of words per week – primarily to assist researchers to develop a habit of writing regularly. That tactic, however, may trigger empty waffle instead of high-quality thought. It's best therefore for supervisors to provide a generalized encouragement to write, without micro-managing the process. But, to repeat, it's axiomatic for historians that putting pen to paper (fingers to keyboards) – and in due course self-editing and revising – are integral components of the entire research process.

Why so? There are both practical and intellectual reasons. For a start, stringing words and paragraphs together to construct a book-length study takes a lot of time. The exercise entails ordering miscellaneous thoughts into a satisfactory sequence, marshalling documented evidence to support the unfolding argument and then punching home a set of original conclusions. It's an arduous art, not an automatic procedure. In other words, the task requires not instant perfectionism, but a readiness to experiment with the art of drafting.

That's because there is a key intellectual as well as practical reason for writing. It constitutes a mechanism for both producing and clarifying thought.[2] Indeed, 'writing is thinking on paper', as the American journalist and educationalist William Zinsser once averred.[3] It's a truly great dictum. Just as spoken language crystallizes instinctive feelings into expressed thoughts, so writing turns swirling thoughts into a considered analysis. History researchers need to think well, as they weld ideas and evidence together, and therefore they need to write – constantly. Part of that process means thinking of the eventual readers (usually defined as 'intelligent outsiders') and ensuring that they are given helpful definitions and signposts. (Further discussed in chapter 7.)

Ironically, while writing is a real aid to thinking, good thinking does not necessarily result in instantly good writing. The process of drafting very often serves to pinpoint arguments and to cue in relevant evidence. Nonetheless, early versions always need later revising and polishing, undertaken in the spirit of the good thinking that launched the writing in the first place.

Some researchers find it helpful to keep an interim research diary, to note down specific details on the research journey. These jottings may include meditations on problems encountered – and ideas of how to resolve them. It can also be useful to list points to stress in the eventual thesis conclusion. However, there's no absolute rule. If keeping a diary becomes just another

---

[2] S. R. Horton, *Thinking through Writing* (London, 1982); L. Katz, *Critical Thinking and Persuasive Writing for Postgraduates* (London, 2018).

[3] W. Zinsser, *On Writing Well* (London, 1976), p. vii.

oppressive chore, then the proposal should be scrapped. The aim is to help, not hinder.

Of course, some evidence needs to be found before an analysis can be built upon it. 'It's a capital mistake to theorize before you have all the evidence', as Conan Doyle once had Sherlock Holmes remark.[4] But there should not be too great a delay between research and writing. In the 'bad old days', history students, who were left without close supervision, often fell into the trap of putting off most of the writing to the final year. Some researchers just fall in love with the archive and the process of research, making 'writing up' seem ever more daunting and distracting. But insights and knowledge are of little use if only one person knows about them. Ensuring that writing up is a continual and developmental process is the best way to avoid a sudden and frequently unworkable shift of gears.

It's worth stressing once more: constant writing and constant thinking are integral to writing a big history project, which entails marshalling complexities. It can't be done quickly. In some science subjects, it's fine to write up experiments at the very end of the process. Then an informed critique of the applied methodology can constitute an important research outcome in its own right. Indeed, it can make a substantive contribution to knowledge, whether the experiment has succeeded or not.

However, historians gain no marks for research that leads to a null-finding. And historical methodologies that do not deliver significant results cut no ice. Thus any notional plans to undertake 'writing up after all the research is done' should be banished entirely from the historians' programme. Such delays mean only that the trail has been allowed to run cold. Writing and thinking keep the research in constant gestation; and, simultaneously, such twin actions allow researchers to find and refine their own styles.[5] (Further 'how-to' advice follows in chapters 7 on writing and 8 on using social media.)

3.5 Summary: fusing inspiration with organization

Grappling with a large-scale history project has been defined as moving a mountain of shifting sand with a teaspoon. Each particular move may seem futile in the face of the whole. Yet the pathway unfolds as the researchers move through the stages systematically, working to flexibly

---

[4] A. Conan Doyle, *A Study in Scarlet* (London, 1887), repr. in *The Penguin Complete Sherlock Holmes* (London, 1981), p. 27.

[5] J. Scott, *Creative Writing and Stylistics: Creative and Critical Approaches* (Basingstoke, 2013); D. N. McCloskey, *Economical Writing: 35 Rules for Clear and Persuasive Prose* (Chicago, Ill., 2019).

negotiated deadlines – and constantly thinking about both the mountain and the pathway.

Supervisors are there to share the task of monitoring constantly and to advise regularly. For them, the process of helping new researchers along the way can also prove fruitful. Postgraduates are invaluable members of the research community. They represent the future of the discipline. So supervisors also enjoy helping the process, as original knowledge is slowly germinated and translated into high-quality publishable material.

Then, in due course, completion will eventually achieve the mind-blowing intellectual combustion, fusing inspiration with organization, which the researcher hoped to achieve from the start.

4. Finding well-attested evidence

SIGNPOST: Relevant to all researchers

A salute to historian Edward Gibbon, master of the pointed footnote, whose six-volume *Decline and Fall of the Roman Empire* (1776) is a 'secondary' source on ancient Rome (written long after the events it is describing), but a 'primary' source (dating from the era in question) for the intellectual life of eighteenth-century Europe.

4.1 Defining primary and secondary sources

A key first step is to distinguish between 'primary' and 'secondary' sources. To undertake historical research, historians need to consult both. 'Primary' sources are defined as all materials drawn from the period of the past under consideration. Those sources may be located in an archive, library, museum, gallery or other depository – or they may be located outdoors, in fields, towns and elsewhere. In the case of some written and visual materials, later editors have made them available in printed collections. If these edited collections have been highly chopped around or otherwise editorially mangled, however, then they lose their pristine primary nature – and have to be treated with caution.

'Secondary' sources, by contrast, are those written or produced after the period which is being studied. These later studies remain vital for understanding the range of debates and for putting primary material into context. Yet statements or images in secondary sources do not constitute infallible 'proof' of an event or trend which happened before the secondary source was produced.

There is no hard-and-fast dividing line between these categories. A weather-beaten piece of furniture offers primary evidence of its original design, while its later state attests to its subsequent use and abuse through time. Moreover, unchanged written sources, which are 'primary' for one purpose, may be 'secondary' for another. It all depends upon the relevant purpose and timeframe. Thus Edmund Gibbon's *Decline and Fall of the Roman Empire* (1776) – one of the greatest historical studies ever written – is a primary source for studies of eighteenth-century historical writings but a secondary source on the development of the Roman Empire. Context is all.

4.2 The broad spectrum of historical evidence

Researching requires keeping alert to the tiniest clues and small telling details, while also scouring the distant horizon for the big picture – and simultaneously assessing all the points in between. It demands tremendous diligence plus imagination – and a willingness to be surprised. So the best combination when approaching new sources is a mix of both excited welcome and critical scepticism.

Sometimes an apparently minor detail encountered on one day will recur in the mind, as later realization dawns that it's not a minor point but a major clue. And the reverse can happen too. Something that seemed conclusive at first sight can then turn out not to be so. The entire process of discovery and evaluation is immensely stimulating for those with the research temperament.

Working throughout a couple of consecutive long days in an archive or museum collection is usually enough to tell embryonic historians whether they do have the interest and capacity for imaginative engagement – or don't. If they decide in the negative, then they are well advised to do something else. There are many other valuable things to do. And it's impossible to fake or to bypass the long-haul process of real research.

As already stressed, everything and anything that survives from the past is potential evidence.[1] Material objects, once largely ignored by historians, have now come into their own.[2] And the same applies to all kinds of visual evidence.[3] There is nothing that cannot be studied: not only words, whether printed or handwritten, but also pottery fragments; textile swatches; collections of bones; DNA records; the contents of old rubbish tips; ruined or surviving buildings; ground plans; all manufactured objects; paintings from cave walls to canvas; photos; films; poems; songs; sayings; myths; fairy tales; jokes … let alone all the evidence constructed or reconstructed by historians, including statistics, graphs, databases … Even the gaps can provide clues: some evidence is known to have existed in the past but hasn't survived.[4] A stirring study by Marisa Fuentes, entitled *Dispossessed Lives: Enslaved Women, Violence, and the Archive*, ingeniously takes the silence of the archive as its starting-point and evidence base.[5] In sum, there is an exhilarating range of options.

Two examples of adventurous use of sources come from students at Royal Holloway, University of London. One was provided by a student who was fascinated by Greek cinema of the 1950s and 1960s. He wanted to use this material as a source for gender and cultural history. It was a fine challenge. Films need scrupulous evaluation, since they are complex team productions, with potentially multiple meanings. The finished versions do not 'speak' for a whole society, although they may dramatize contemporary preoccupations.[6]

[1] University of London's Institute of Historical Research's website provides great guidance: see <https://www.history.ac.uk> [accessed 29 April 2021]. See also M. Drake and R. Finnegan, *Sources and Methods for Family and Community Historians: a Handbook* (Cambridge, 1997); S. Porter, *Exploring Urban History: Sources for Local Historians* (London, 1990); P. Carter and K. Thompson, *Sources for Local Historians* (Chichester, 2005); C. Armstrong, *Using Non-Textual Sources: a Historian's Guide* (London, 2015).

[2] See A. Gerritson and G. Riello (ed.), *Writing Material Culture History* (London, 2014); L. Hannan and S. Longair, *History through Material Culture* (Manchester, 2017); K. Harvey (ed.), *History and Material Culture: a Student's Guide to Approaching Alternative Sources* (London, 2017).

[3] P. Burke, *Eyewitnessing: the Uses of Images as Historical Evidence* (London, 2001); L. Jordanova, *The Look of the Past: Visual and Material Evidence in Historical Practice* (Cambridge, 2012).

[4] On missing or concealed evidence, see V. Johnson, S. Fowler and D. Thomas, *The Silence of the Archive* (London, 2017).

[5] M. J. Fuentes, *Dispossessed Lives: Enslaved Women, Violence, and the Archive* (Philadelphia, Pa., 2016).

[6] J. Chapman, *Film and History* (Basingstoke, 2013); R. Rosenstone, *Visions of the Past: the Challenge of Film to Our Idea of History* (Cambridge, Mass., 1995); and National Archives: <https://web.archive.org/web/20211227112935/https://www.nationalarchives.gov.uk/education/focuson/film/introduction/> [accessed 27 Dec. 2021].

In this case, Achilleas Hadjikyriacou's study of filmic representations of Greek masculinity made an excellent dissertation. Moreover, he then extended his researches into a PhD, now published as a scintillating monograph.[7]

Another case-study came from a student who declared a disdain for history but a passion for his football club. After some discussion, it became clear that here was the kernel of an innovative dissertation. Many football clubs have substantial records, including documents and memorabilia, which are often seriously under-studied.[8] In this case, Southampton F.C. welcomed the student researcher warmly. He not only consulted their records but also, while mingling with fans on the terraces, made an audio-tape of their chants and songs. This evidence was then used to explore the origins and nature of crowd participation, aided by testimonies from veteran supporters. The resultant study, framed in the then emerging field of the history of sport, broke fresh ground. And the student found a veritable labour of love. These days, his study would be ideal for multi-media web publication. (A positive hint, should he ever read this *Guide*!)

In other words, it's clear that the sources for historical research are by no means exclusively found in local or national archives – treasure troves, as they so often prove to be.[9] All manner of public galleries, museums and repositories have relevant holdings. These days, there are also new digitized collections, which are opening up exciting possibilities.[10] They allow researchers to search and use previously inaccessible and non-standardized data.[11] (The status of these curated sources for digital history further complicates the boundaries between primary and secondary material – as discussed in further detail below.) And there also remain sundry private collections, some explored, some still unexplored. All these sources can be compared and contrasted. There is no requirement for researchers to stick to just one type of evidence or just one research location.

---

[7] A. Hadjikyriacou, *Masculinity and Gender in Greek Cinema: 1949–67* (New York, 2013).

[8] But see J. Walvin, *The People's Game: the History of Football Revisited* (London, 2014) and P. Brown, *Savage Enthusiasm: a History of Football Fans* (Durham, 2017). Moreover, some football clubs, such as Leyton Orient in East London, include local history projects among their outreach work in the local community.

[9] See the exemplary overview provided by the National Archives: <https://web.archive .org/web/20220322130731/https://www.nationalarchives.gov.uk/help-with-your-research/> [accessed 22 March 2022].

[10] An invaluable resource for London's legal, social and cultural history is *The Proceedings of the Old Bailey: London's Central Criminal Court, 1674–1913 online*, co-directed by Tim Hitchcock and Robert Shoemaker: <https://www.oldbaileyonline.org> [accessed 29 April 2021].

[11] See, eg, S. Tickell, *Shoplifting in Eighteenth-Century England* (London, 2018).

Up until recently, there existed a certain archival snobbery. It implied that manuscript documents were the only authentic focus for research. And that attitude began for good reasons. Many of the earliest histories were based upon 'scissors-and-paste' methods. Snippets were extracted from published works by others and then reassembled. So the move to study original sources in archives was a key part of history's professionalization.[12] It advanced the subject from repetition to originality. And documentary research continues to play a vital role. Yet nowadays the nature of each archive needs to be evaluated carefully. In particular, official sources often need to be amplified by other materials. A traditional reliance upon state archives tended to restrict attention to the concerns of the state, and to tempt historians into reproducing the views of the powerful and privileged.

These days, however, diversification is encouraging a new focus upon previously excluded people and places. Indeed, the widening of the source base is generating a much more realistic and pluralist model of past societies, enabling an exciting plurality of voices and experiences to be examined and incorporated.

Usually, archivists and most other guardians of historical collections, who often undertake research themselves, are tremendously helpful in suggesting sources. They are experts on the materials they preserve. And while there are archival 'discoveries' to be made, historians readily acknowledge that in almost all instances, the archivists were there first – for example, when cataloguing collections and making them findable. But research vigilance remains essential. Sometimes old listings have vague or incomplete entries, which need probing. There are often unstudied items inside larger bundles (such as boxes of legal documents). There are newly found materials, such as those at archaeological digs. Or newly created materials, like oral history interviews. And much bulk evidence has not yet been digitized and made available for systematic analysis.

Both researching and cataloguing thus remain perennial works-in-progress. Not only does the length of the past continue to increase steadily, but the range of materials accepted as valid sources is continually growing. And, of course, there are always new cross-connections to be made that may transform separate bits of evidence into something wholly new.

---

[12] M. Friedrich, *The Birth of the Archive: the History of Knowledge*, transl. J. N. Dillon (Ann Arbor, Mich., 2018); A. Farge, *The Allure of the Archives*, transl. T. Scott-Railton (New Haven, Conn., 2013); and a meditation on resources for cultural historians, in C. Steedman, *Dust* (Manchester, 2001).

4.3 Evaluating sources for a specific project

Researchers can start with an idea or a question, and seek out relevant sources to provide an answer. Or, just as productively, they can start from the other end – in a collection or archive. It's most common, however, to identify a general area of interest and then to devise questions while auditing different materials, until a sufficient combination has been assembled to make a start.

Most studies use a combination of many sources, with one or two major collections at their core. Further issues are raised by the rise of digital sources. For 'born digital' topics, the problem is now an abundance rather than scarcity of relevant sources. And for themes which can be illuminated by large, machine-searchable collections (such as newspapers and other print material), the challenge is to mesh their findings with archival research into non-digitized material. Researchers, aided by their supervisors, strive to find the right balance.

Evaluating the evidence is a normal part of the process. It's good to mull things over carefully. How can these or those sources best be used? Are they helpful for the project? What information can be created by comparing different records? What patterns, if any, are emerging? What story is leaping from the record? Or what analysis is not leaping, but needing careful construction and consideration? From time to time, researchers talk, rather romantically, about giving unknown people from the past 'a voice'. Yet the research process entails much more than finding and repeating past testimonies. Evidence does not speak for itself. It's the historians who are reconstructing and analysing the past.

It happens sometimes that researchers refer to 'sampling' their evidence in the loose, non-technical sense of that verb. However, it's best to be precise. Regular sampling of a large dataset entails a completely systematic selection process, such as homing in upon one in every five items of information, or one in ten, twenty, thirty or whatever. Such procedures can be immensely helpful, provided that the sources are suitably detailed and consistent. Indeed, a systematic sample may be the only way of analysing really huge collections of data, which otherwise would be too large for total inspection.[13] Meanwhile, an overview of diverse and non-standardized sources (a common procedure) is best described not as a 'sample' but as a 'survey'.

Hunches can also be helpful. It's good to cast the nets widely. To look for sources in unexpected places, and to use unanticipated search criteria.

[13] M. J. Slonim, *Sampling: a Quick, Reliable Guide to Practical Statistics* (New York, 1960).

This tactic has been described as 'going fishing'. Sometimes a researcher will strike it lucky by finding sources that can, unexpectedly, illuminate a known research question from a different angle. For example, if a rare early pamphlet has been bound both separately and with a collection of other pamphlets in a library, then it's good to order the collection, just to see what happenstance will provide. Similarly, at the start of searching an online database, it can be instructive to try some random searches, to see what is or is not available.

Meanwhile, the technology of search, research and analysis is changing all the time. Even thirty years ago, most historians consumed their sources in the form in which they were created – they read them as books and letters. But, as these materials are turned into digital objects, it is now possible to explore word frequency or changing linguistic forms – to undertake a process of 'distant reading'.[14] This development has expanded historians' toolkit, but also challenged them to make sense of technically complex systems. (For more on this pertinent theme, see chapter 6.)

But again, it's vital to keep a mental cost-benefit as a firm check on the use of time. It is easy to become too fond of rooting around in archives or – these days – searching on the web or assessing digitized collections, to the detriment of actually analysing the evidence. As more and more materials are kept, in one format or another, the problems of abundance have replaced the old problems of scarcity of source materials.[15] For that reason, the discipline of regular writing, alongside searching for fresh sources, is designed to keep the endless-discovery bug under control.

4.4 The prosaic necessity for accurate note-taking

Throughout, it's vital to keep careful notes of what has been examined and what methodologies (if any) have been used. At first, it seems easy to remember exactly what was found and where. But researchers beware! Memory fades. As a result, researchers, especially in their early days, often find that they have to retrace their footsteps to find some telling item that

---

[14] F. Moretti, *Graphs, Maps, Trees: Abstract Models for a Literary History* (London, 2005); J. Goodwin and J. Holbo (ed.), *Reading Graphs, Maps and Trees: Responses to Franco Moretti* (Anderson, S.C., 2011).

[15] Among a fast-growing literature, see N. E. Pearce (ed.), *Archival Choices: Managing the Historical Record in an Age of Abundance* (Lexington, Mass., 1984); R. Rosenzweig, 'Scarcity or abundance? Preserving the past in a digital era', *American Historical Review*, cviii (2003), 735–62; D. J. Cohen, 'The future of preserving the past', *Journal of Heritage Stewardship*, ii (2005), 6–19; J. E. Olsen, *Database Archiving: How to Keep Lots of Data for a Very Long Time* (London, 2010).

was earlier glimpsed but which then mysteriously disappeared. The mantra remains: take fully detailed notes, exactly as the research unfolds.

Such information needs to include full reference details to the source and its location, and full information about the page or folio (or any other identifying internal detail) to indicate where specific information is to be found. It can also be useful to keep a note of the date when any given set of sources was examined. (That point applies particularly when studying rare materials which are not commonly available.) At an early stage, researchers should also decide on their preferred strategy for data management and footnoting. (Detailed advice follows in chapter 6.)

The sources themselves must always be treated with the utmost respect. That proposition is axiomatic. Sources must not be mangled, spoiled, misquoted or destroyed. Organized collections of material will have rules and instructions about looking after them. Those should be followed to the letter. Moreover, any researchers who have the good fortune to get access to historical sources which are still held in private hands should follow the same procedural rules. The research materials need to be kept clean, dry, unscuffed and ink-free. Pencils rather than pens should be used for note-taking, and it's helpful to leave a notice to alert future researchers to do likewise. Such actions underline the value of all archives, no matter what their provenance.

It goes without saying that all documents or other research materials should be left essentially unaltered, although, in the case of private holdings, it is acceptable to sift very scattered materials (such as loose letters or other documents) into chronological order, if asked to do so by the owners (and if there is no apparent reason to their miscellaneous preservation). However, no irremovable changes should be made. Historians are not archivists, and well-meaning changes to a collection can frequently do more damage than good. Re-ordering a collection of receipts, or using paper clips or acid-based paper folders, can easily destroy valuable evidence.

By the way, it's good to encourage holders of private collections to deposit copies in the public domain – or to deposit the material on loan. Both those options can help to share the responsibility of caring for unique historical sources. Not all archives or depositories are equally interested in acquiring new materials (cataloguing and storage costs money), but many are – so it's always worth exploring options.

All this effort at accuracy is needed because, when presenting a thesis or publishing original research, it is expected that full identifying documentation will appear in the accompanying notes (either as footnotes or endnotes). The point is to indicate clearly the trail of evidence. In that way, others can, if need be, follow and cross-check everything.

Hence the presence of notes declares that there's nothing to hide. The sources have been used fairly and honestly. Other researchers, investigating the same materials, might interpret them differently. But they should not be able to find any factual error or mishandling. (And see chapter 6 on using online internet-archiving to save accurate web citations, which otherwise risk becoming degraded or disappearing entirely.)

At this point, it's worth noting the separate status of textbooks and studies for a general readership. They constitute a different category of historical writing, without the attachment of detailed references. Such works are usually entrusted to established scholars, whose good faith is taken as read. In all cases, however, readers should still maintain a critical stance. Historical studies thrive not upon established authority but upon evidence and debate.

4.5 *The vital need for well-attested evidence*

To repeat: pronouncements without tried and tested evidence in support are but assertions, no matter how loudly they are proclaimed – or how eminent is the authority behind the pronouncement. Citing sources is thus not a pernickety detail. It's the clear presentation of the building blocks of knowledge.

Rarely, the implicit rules are broken. In such disastrous cases, researchers who are reliably shown to have misquoted, invented, misrepresented, garbled or faked the source material lose the respect of their colleagues. Sadly, one example was provided by Joseph J. Ellis, the American historian who won a Pulitzer Prize in 2001 for his account of the American Founding Fathers. It transpired that he had fictionalized his own past. He had falsely claimed that he'd been an anti-war activist after having fought for his country in Vietnam as a paratrooper, before serving on the staff of the US commander General Westmoreland.[16] Upon discovery, Ellis apologized profusely. And, intriguingly, the syndrome, whereby people falsely claim to have participated in notable historical moments, is not uncommon.[17] It's a form of over-identification, possibly even hiding a complex retrospective guilt for inaction. Nonetheless, there's no doubt that the episode was deeply disappointing, not least to Ellis's students who had been beguiled by his tales.

[16] 'Historian fakes his own history', *The Guardian*, 20 June 2001: <https://www.the guardian.com/world/2001/jun/20/humanities.highereducation> [accessed 25 Mar. 2022]

[17] Numerous false Vietnam claims are cited in B. G. Burkett and G. Whitley, *Stolen Valour: How the Vietnam Generation Was Robbed of Its Heroes and Its History* (Dallas, Tex., 1998).

Other scholars fall into egregious errors through simple ignorance and lack of care. The well-known feminist author, Naomi Wolf, for instance, wrote a major book premised on the mistaken belief that the verdict 'Death Recorded' at the Old Bailey law-courts was clear evidence of the execution of large numbers of homosexual men in nineteenth-century London. In fact, the terse entry, first used in 1823, actually meant that the stark sentence was noted as a preliminary to its commutation to a lesser penalty by the judge. The exposure of this error resulted in an embarrassing public controversy, and forced Wolf's publisher to recall the full print-run of the volume on the eve of publication.[18]

Thus, researchers as well as their research data may need critical checking. Understanding the limitations to knowledge is also part of research. Some challenges cannot be met directly, or can be answered only obliquely. There is also a world of half-truths and untruths, which lend themselves to study too. But the critical evaluation of evidence, both reliable and unreliable, forms the core basis of historical thought.

Among philosophical critics known as postmodernists,[19] there was an intellectual movement during the last four decades of the twentieth century to interrogate more fully the claims to empirical truth at the heart of history-writing. These debates had a galvanizing impact. Postmodernism won greatest support among literary theorists. Yet it also prodded historians to interrogate more carefully the nature of their sources, and the 'truth' of the claims they make.[20] Overall, the postmodernist approach helped to foster a healthy scepticism about standard claims of power and authority. It greatly expanded the notion of evidence. And it drew attention to the ways in which language is often coded with deeper meanings, thus warning researchers not to take all documents too literally.

Yet, at its most extreme, postmodernist thought implied that humans cannot know about the past in any real sense. It challenged the role of memory in the present, and also the tangible legacy of material circumstances over time. In sum, it took the subjectivity of knowledge too far. If the past was

[18] N. Sayej, '"I don't feel humiliated": Naomi Wolf on historical inaccuracy controversy', *The Guardian*, 21 June 2019: <https://www.theguardian.com/books/2019/jun/21/naomi-wolf-book-outrages-new-york> [accessed 29 April 2021].

[19] H. Bertens, *The Idea of the Postmodern: a History* (London, 1995); P. Anderson, *The Origins of Postmodernity* (London, 1998); T. Woods, *Beginning Postmodernism* (Manchester, 1999, 2002).

[20] For postmodernist approaches, see H. V. White, *The Content of Form: Narrative Discourse and Historical Representation* (London, 1973); K. Jenkins, *Re-Thinking History* (London, 1991, 2003); C. G. Brown, *Postmodernism for Historians* (Harlow, 2005); A. Munslow, *Narrative and History* (Basingstoke, 2007).

essentially unknowable by historians, there would be no way of evaluating whether one historical claim is more accurate than any other. For instance, there'd be no way of rebutting (say) Holocaust denial.[21] Indeed, there'd be no way of knowing anything definite about any past event.[22] The utmost that could be admitted would be a pervasive stance of sceptical doubt.

Life, however, would be impossible lived in such a state of total nescience. People generally and historians professionally do manage to learn a great deal about bygone ages. They also convey their knowledge to later generations. Researchers constantly evaluate, interpret and knit together many different forms of checked and tested evidence, in the light of evolving debates and pooled research, as well as their own considered analysis. And in the wider culture, doubters are now being challenged in turn. Indeed, by 2020 the habit of defining the current era as an 'Age of Postmodernity' was fast disappearing – even if there is no generally agreed alternative as to what prevails instead.[23] (There is also a receding trust in the concept of one earlier period of uniform 'Modernity', too, but that debate is taking longer to unwind.)

4.6 Summary: generating knowledge

In sum, the fact that knowledge is often imperfect and always open to challenge does not mean that there is no knowledge. There are many gradations between certainties, probabilities, possibilities, uncertainties, doubts, improbabilities and outright impossibilities. The sum is always a work-in-progress, created, selected and debated by humans, on behalf of their fellow humans.

[21] On Holocaust denial, see D. Lipstadt, *Denying the Holocaust: the Growing Assault on Truth and Memory* (New York, 1993); D. Lipstadt, *History on Trial: My Day in Court with a Holocaust Denier* (New York, 2005); and R. J. Evans, *Telling Lies about Hitler: the Holocaust, History and the David Irving Trial* (London, 2002).

[22] C. Norris, *What's Wrong with Postmodernism: Critical Theory and the Ends of Philosophy* (London, 1990); K. Windschuttle, *The Killing of History: How Literary Critics and Social Theorists Are Murdering Our Past* (New York, 1996); R. J. Evans, *In Defence of History* (London, 1997); G. Myerson, *Ecology and the End of Postmodernism* (Cambridge, 2001); B. Kuźniarz, *Farewell to Postmodernism: Social Theories of the Late Left*, transl. S. Bill (Frankfurt am Main, 2015).

[23] See J. T. Nealon, *Post-Postmodernism: Or, the Cultural Logic of 'Just-in-Time' Capitalism* (Stanford, Calif., 2012) and N. A. Raab, *The Humanities in Transition from Postmodernism into the Digital Age* (London, 2020).

5. Probing sources and methodologies

SIGNPOST: Relevant to all researchers

A salute to historical detectives everywhere.

5.1 How good are the sources?

Historians are very often asked: 'What are the sources?'. Yet that query should really be paired with: 'Are the sources good enough for your project?'. Using evidence from the past entails understanding its strengths as well as its biases, limitations and omissions. There's thus a constant mental dialogue between analysing sources and building conclusions. Good historians, like good detectives, need to start somewhere but also keep an open mind. So they should both follow and challenge the evidence.[1] If, during a multi-year

[1] On that two-way theme, see Anon., *The Historian as Detective: Essays on Evidence* (London, 1969); plus R. B. Browne and L. A. Kreiser (ed.), *The Detective as Historian:*

project, researchers have not either confirmed a previously shaky view or formulated a valid new one, then they have not been doing their job. Historians need constantly to revisit their assumptions and, if need be, to adapt their views as things develop. Such refinements are the essence of historical scholarship.

Interrogating the sources does not imply that evidence from the past is being blamed or belittled. That's not the intention at all. Historical sources simply are as they survive – or as, in some cases, they can be reconstructed. Yet they all need to be used with real care. The golden rule is to play fair with the evidence.

As already stressed – and it is worth stressing again – falsifying data, misquoting sources, selecting only positive information, hiding unfavourable evidence or mangling research techniques are all supreme academic sins.

Critical reflections upon the nature of the evidence usually appear near the start of all research studies. Sometimes a source audit may be summarized briefly, while at other times, it may command an entire chapter or more. Such commentaries are not pedantry. In fact, exploring the strong and weak points of specific sorts of sources can turn into a fascinating exercise in itself. And, once complete, the audit establishes the basis for the study that follows. Indeed, most supervisors ask researchers to start with this process precisely to produce an overview that sets the scene both knowledgeably and critically.

At this point, it's worth emphasizing that researchers should think laterally and imaginatively about how to deploy and interrogate the evidence. Materials need not only be used for the purposes for which they were created. For example, historians of religious change in sixteenth-century England examined the preambles to ordinary citizens' wills. The aim was to detect a shift in expressions of popular adherence from Catholicism to Protestantism. Of course, some testators might have relied upon friends or clerical advisors when making wills; but, in such cases, it was the helpers who were reflecting the shift. On the other hand, will-making may have remained throughout a matter of unchanging cultural ritual.[2] Hence the evidence was suggestive but not conclusive. It's a classic case of rival interpretations of a change for

---

History and Art in Historical Crime Fiction, Vol. 1 (Bowling Green, Ohio, 2000); Browne and Kreiser (ed.), *Detective as Historian, Vol. II* (Newcastle upon Tyne, 2009).

[2] See C. J. Litzenberger, *The English Reformation and the Laity: Gloucestershire, 1540–80* (Cambridge, 1997), pp. 168–78; E. Duffy, *The Stripping of the Altars: Traditional Religion in England, c.1400–c.1580* (London, 1992, 2005), pp. 515–21; J. D. Alsop, 'Religious preambles in early modern English wills as formulae', *Journal of Ecclesiastical History*, xl (1989), 19–27.

which there was no one single definitive source. But it's also a creative way of considering how big policy changes at a national level may have impacted upon daily lives.

5.2 The preliminary source check

Provenance

It's always worth starting with a basic check. What is the provenance of any given category of source material? Who created it and why? How has it survived from its original state through to the present day? How well authenticated is it? Has it been amended or changed over time? (Usually yes.) Has the entire collection any in-built biases – perhaps reflecting past racist and/or sexist attitudes?[3] Was the evidence amassed for a particular purpose – often as an archive of record, but sometimes as a collection for propaganda purposes? All these resources provide real and effective documentation, but they are not neutral lenses upon the past.

Usually all items that have been assembled in public archives, libraries, galleries and museums have been authenticated before they are incorporated into a collection. That process does not mean that their interpretation is beyond debate (far from it), but it does confirm that all materials are genuinely what they purport to be. However, a small proportion of mis-attributed items or subsequent fabrications may also creep into the record. There are also processes of restoration, whose impact needs to be recognized. On a grand scale, visitors to present-day Bruges[4] or the palace of Knossos in Crete[5] might think that they are viewing a well-preserved medieval city or a Cretan archaeological marvel, but they are actually witnessing the impact of zealous (some might say over-zealous) restoration by nineteenth- and twentieth-century enthusiasts. Their handiwork is thus, at one and the same time, real historical evidence and 'fake'.

If there is any doubt, the matter should be checked and rechecked. The entire journey of all materials from formation to preservation to research usage needs interrogation. The same rule applies to material in private

---

[3] T. Shellam and J. Cruickshank, 'Critical archives: an introduction', *Journal of Colonialism and Colonial History*, xx (2019), *Project MUSE*, doi: 10.1353/cch.2019.0017.

[4] See J. McDonald, *Bruges: Historic Walking Guides*, ed. Z. Wildsmith (Durham, 2009); 'Just How Medieval Is Bruges?' (2020): <https://en.tripadvisor.com.hk/ShowTopic-g188671-i448-k12710656-o10-Some_travelers_claim_that_Bruges_is_a_fake_medieval_city-Bruges_West_Flanders_Province.html> [accessed 29 April 2021].

[5] J. A. MacGillivray, *Minotaur: Sir Arthur Evans and the Archaeology of the Minoan Myth* (London, 1997); N. Marinatos, *Sir Arthur Evans and Minoan Crete: Creating the Vision of Knossos* (London, 2014).

holdings. It is unusual for individuals to go to immense trouble to fabricate authentic-seeming sources. But it is easy enough for family folklore to attribute spurious age and authority to the disorderly contents of an attic.

Cases of documentary and archaeological fakes are all too well known. These are sometimes perpetrated for motives of financial gain – or to substantiate a controversial theory. In 2005–6, that allegedly prompted the historian, Martin Allen, to insert twenty-nine fabricated documents, relating to Britain's policies in the Second World War, into The National Archives.[6] Researchers should accordingly beware! The first requirement is to check (however swiftly) the provenance of all sources.

Furthermore, the frequent repetition of items of knowledge as known 'facts' does not automatically guarantee their accuracy. At times, errors can slip through the net. Falsehoods can be repeated so frequently that they are assumed to be true, until exposed as erroneous, thereby seriously wrong-footing all the experts who had relied upon their veracity. An example can be found in the alleged popular riots against calendar reform in England in September 1752. Many historians had repeated the story. But Robert Poole's meticulous research revealed that the popular riots, when people allegedly shouted 'Give us back our eleven days', did not happen.[7] They were a later myth, built on assumptions that the poor were superstitious, credulous and automatically hostile to change. Such phoney facts are known as 'factoids', in an eloquent term first coined by Norman Mailer in 1973.[8] So again, the message is simple. Facts too may prove dubious; and, if in any doubt, researchers should check and double-check – again.

Reliability

A source or group of sources may still be authentic but not necessarily reliable in the sense of being precise or accurate. Materials from the past have no historic duty to be anything other than what they were. A song about 'happy times' is no proof that times were actually happy, either when the song was first written, or in all the subsequent eras when it was sung again. Yet it's significant that songs to happy times are written – and repeated in

---

[6] For documents discovered to be forgeries in the custody of The National Archives, see <https://discovery.nationalarchives.gov.uk/details/r/C16525> [accessed 29 April 2021].

[7] The error was ably exposed in R. Poole, *Time's Alteration: Calendar Reform in Early Modern England* (London, 1998), pp. 1–18, 159–78; and Poole, '"Give us our eleven days!" Calendar reform in eighteenth-century England', *Past & Present*, cxlix (1995), 95–139.

[8] N. Mailer, *Marilyn: a Biography* (London, 1973, 2012), p. 9. In addition, the term is sometimes used, chiefly in the USA, to denote a trivial fact or 'factlet': see <https://en.wikipedia.org/wiki/Factoid> [accessed 29 April 2021].

the repertoire. Their contents, their music and their performance history (if known) can all be decoded. In that way, the history of songs constitutes a very fruitful field of enquiry, provided that it is recalled that survival rates for this sort of ephemera are patchy – and that song lyrics are not taken as the equivalent of declarations on oath.[9] That latter point applies to much subjective documentation from the past. Statements which are not made on oath have no obligation to be accurate; and even sworn affidavits may lie.

Generally, it's enough for historians to flag the difficulties in interpreting subjective testimonies, and to take such challenges into account when interpreting the material. Such assessments are the stuff of interpretation. The subjective nature of many documentary sources is not an insurmountable problem as such, but it is an issue which needs to be handled with real thought and care. How to deal with often complexly flawed evidence is one of the primary challenges for historians.

Another problem may also emerge when 'primary' sources are subsequently edited – and when the originals have disappeared, thus removing the chance for checking. For the most part historians have to take editorial accuracy on trust. Yet, if there is any doubt, then they should immediately accept that the source is no longer a valid 'primary' source but a doctored, later concoction. One classic example was the removal of religious fervour from the mid seventeenth-century *Memoirs of Edmund Ludlow* by the late seventeenth-century editor, who was a militant rationalist. Only very much later was a manuscript version discovered. A cross-check between the two versions was salutary. It showed that the editor had given the *Memoirs* a markedly secular tone, which was long, but wrongly, accepted as authentic.[10]

Digital sources have also introduced further problems. Take the example of the Burney Collection of Seventeenth- and Eighteenth-Century Newspapers. The process of making them available online has built in sundry biases. First amassed in the late eighteenth and early nineteenth centuries, the collection was acquired by the British Library in 1818, and slowly augmented by additional sources. But from the start the collection was substantially biased towards London. For preservation reasons, it was then microfilmed in the 1950s, greatly enhancing its availability. However, those enthusiastically searching the contents made only little acknowledgement of their metropolitan bias.

[9] R. Palmer, *The Sound of History: Songs and Social Comment* (Oxford, 1988).
[10] B. Worden, *Roundhead Reputations: the English Civil Wars and the Passions of Posterity* (London, 2001).

Then, in the early twenty-first century, the collection was translated into a new digital version via a process called Optical Character Recognition (OCR). This automatically generates a searchable electronic text.[11] But, sad to say, the OCR of print from the seventeenth and eighteenth centuries is notoriously prone to error. Less than 50% of semantically significant words in the online version of the Burney Collection are transcribed accurately.[12] And that figure rises for text printed in italics or in tabular form. The Burney Collection is so substantial that most keyword searches will still produce useable results. But historians must get to grips with the problems generated by its metropolitan bias and with the current technological limitations upon word recognition. Consequently, the universal motto is: researchers be aware!

Typicality

With all sources, it's also helpful to pose the question as to whether their evidence is likely to be commonplace or highly unusual. Again, it doesn't matter which it is, as long as the implications are fully taken into account. Otherwise, there is a danger of generalizing from something that is in fact a rarity; or, conversely, of taking something as exceptional which was actually commonplace.

Assessing typicality is not always easy, especially in the case of obscure and fragmentary materials. Yet it's always helpful, wherever possible, to check one source against many comparable examples, to gain a sense of the genre. And it's equally good to acknowledge difficulties when using the said evidence.

Keeping a sense of proportion is particularly relevant when supporting references for something previously unknown can be found relatively rapidly by keyword searching of digitized data. It's good that such methods can both find and contextualize a new piece of information. For example, the unorthodox historian E. P. Thompson – a great searcher after new sources – startled his fellow researchers in the 1970s with a lecture on eighteenth-century wife sales. These *de facto* popular divorces, forbidden by both church and state, were very rarely mentioned. Yet they did occur. Once Thompson had alerted the research community, then others found that their eyes were

---

[11] A. Prescott, 'Searching for Dr Johnson: the digitization of the Burney Newspaper Collection', in *Travelling Chronicles: News and Newspapers from the Early Modern Period to the Eighteenth Century*, ed. G. Brantzaeg et al. (Leiden, 2018), pp. 51–71.

[12] S. Turner, T. Muñoz and P. H. Ros, 'Measuring mass text digitization quality and usefulness: lessons learned from assessing the OCR accuracy of the British Library's Nineteenth-Century Online Newspaper Archive', *D-Lib Magazine*, xv (July/August 2009): <http://www.dlib.org/dlib/july09/munoz/07munoz.html> [accessed 29 April 2021].

opened to new cases, many being recorded in the provincial newspapers. The topic was thus well and truly brought in from the cold.[13] Yet it is still helpful for researchers to indicate that wife sales were far from commonplace, chiefly because of their problematic legal status. The couples settling their matrimonial affairs in this manner (usually by joint agreement) were taking a calculated risk to gain public acknowledgement of their changed status. A sense of scale, in other words, reveals the full meaning.

5.3 The close source critique

Context

Having looked generically at a source or group of research materials, it's then useful to make precise checks. Step one advises that all evidence be put into its context of time and place. One example makes the point. Finding a sheet of paper inscribed with the words 'William, son of John Shakespeare' would not get a researcher very far. But locating them in the parish book of Holy Trinity, Stratford-upon-Avon, dated 26 April 1564, provides good evidence of the baptism of the world's most famous William Shakespeare.

The document in question contains four words in Latin: 'Gulielmus filius Johannis Shakspere'. A later hand marked the entry with three inked crosses. It was an endearing sign of research excitement, although today it would rightly attract the wrath of archivists. Hence it can be reliably assumed that Shakespeare was born some time very shortly before his baptism on 26 April. The precise date, however, remains unknown. (A patriotic tradition dating back to the eighteenth century ascribes it to 23 April – St George's Day.)

Style or register

Step two requires a full understanding of the source's characteristic style or 'register', in the terminology of literary scholarship. At a very basic level, there are obvious differences in written texts between fiction and non-fiction. Poems, stories and songs are not intended to be taken literally. And within the ranks of non-fiction, there are many different types of writings, and levels of specificity. Private thoughts expressed casually, in (say) letters and diaries, do not necessarily constitute people's final considered views.

---

[13] S. P. Menafee, *Wives for Sale: an Ethnographic Study of British Popular Divorce* (Oxford, 1981); E. P. Thompson, 'The sale of wives', in his *Customs in Common* (London, 1991), pp. 404–68; B. Drummond, *Frolicksome Women and Troublesome Wives: Wife Selling in England* (London, 2018).

Researchers thus have to allow for human variability. Guidebooks also helpfully review the common characteristics of personal sources, such as autobiographies,[14] diaries,[15] reported speech[16] and letters.[17]

Again, the historic documentation relating to William Shakespeare provides a salient example. When his will bequeathed to his wife Anne Hathaway their 'second best bed', he was not comparing her to a summer's day. He was leaving her a specific item of household furniture. It can be debated whether the legacy was a considered snub or a tender personal testimonial or a utilitarian disposal of family assets or just a casual after-thought (given that this bequest was visibly a late addition to the will, interpolated between two lines of an already written text).[18] But the testator's motivation was not specified. In other words, the legal register provided terse wording for a specific purpose, differing utterly from the poetic register, which can be anything from closely observed to rapturous to nonsensical.

It's thus for the researcher to determine how a given source can or cannot be used (and to defend that decision, if challenged) – and that point applies whatever the nature of the surviving evidence from the past.

---

[14] J. D. Popkin, *History, Historians and Autobiography* (Chicago, Ill., 2005); N. G. Adamson, *Notable Women in World History: a Guide to Recommended Biographies and Autobiographies* (London, 1998); J. Burnett (ed.), *Annals of Labour: Autobiographies of Working-Class People, 1820–1920* (London, 1974); and many other compilations.

[15] A. Ponsonby, *English Diaries: a Review of English Diaries from the Sixteenth to the Twentieth Century …* (New York, 1923, 1971); J. S. Batts, *British Manuscript Diaries of the Nineteenth Century: an Annotated Listing* (Totowa, N.J., 1976); H. Blodgett, *Centuries of Female Days: Englishwomen's Private Diaries* (Gloucester, 1989); and a magnificent collected set by M. Bird (ed.), *The Diary of Mary Hardy, 1773–1809: V vols* (Kingston upon Thames, 2013), with accompanying essays in M. Bird, *Mary Hardy and Her World, 1773–1809: IV vols* (Kingston upon Thames, 2020).

[16] See A. Fox and S. Woolf (ed.), *The Spoken Word: Oral Culture in Britain, 1500–1850* (Manchester, 2002) and guide to oratory in B. MacArthur (ed.), *The Penguin Book of Historic Speeches* (London, 1995).

[17] On this source, see E. T. Bannet, *Empire of Letters: Letter Manuals and Transatlantic Correspondence, 1680–1820* (Cambridge, 2005); S. E. Whyman, *The Pen and the People: English Letter Writers, 1660–1800* (Oxford, 2009); and L. Hannan, 'The imperfect letter-writer: escaping the advice manuals', in P. J. Corfield and L. Hannan (ed.), *Hats Off, Gentlemen! Changing Arts of Communication in the Eighteenth Century/Arts de communiquer au dix-huitième siècle* (Paris, 2017), pp. 53–72.

[18] J. Rogers, *The Second Best Bed: Shakespeare's Will in a New Light* (Westport, Conn., 1993); M. S. Hedges, *The Second Best Bed: In Search of Anne Hathaway* (Lewes, 2000); G. Greer, *Shakespeare's Wife* (London, 2007).

Contents

After all these necessary preliminaries, researchers can at last savour the full contents of the sources in question. Every last detail may be important. As PJC's former research supervisor Jack Fisher used to say: squeeze every last drop of juice from the lemon.

Possibilities, however, always remain bounded by the availability of evidence – and by the time and methods available for analysis. Again, it's worth repeating those salient points. Some things are genuinely lost from history. So, without fresh finds, Shakespeare's actual birth date will remain unknown; and his attitude to his wife, when making his will, also remains a matter of conjecture.

Of course, it's always possible that new discoveries may be made. A good place to look would be within the only partially catalogued sixteenth-century legal records. Meanwhile, all new finds and claims about Shakespeare will be subject to extra-stringent checking and criticism from the world's array of enthusiastic bardologists.[19]

Considering the question of missing sources more broadly, some big fields of research will entail finding careful mechanisms to work around major absences. When the British government gave up many of its colonial possessions in the 1950s, it destroyed many historical records – literally burning them or dumping them in the sea.[20] The motivation may have been either to avoid the effort and cost of preservation; or, more deviously, to sidestep the danger of any subsequent allegations of political malfeasance.

Either way, historians analysing the colonial era will need to proceed without those documents, but in the knowledge that they once existed. As in so many cases, ingenuity is the best response to challenge.

5.4 Choosing appropriate methodologies: general principles

'Methodology' is an abstraction which refers to the different research methods, whether straightforward or technically complex, which all historians adopt.[21] It's high time to demystify the term, which is not especially lovely but is useful. Earlier generations of British historians

---

[19] For burgeoning interest in 'the Bard', see C. LaPorte, *The Victorian Cult of Shakespeare: Bardology in the Nineteenth Century* (Cambridge, 2020) and also C. Woo, *Romantic Actors and Bardolatry: Performing Shakespeare from Garrick to Kean* (New York, 2008).

[20] S. Shohei. '"Operation Legacy": Britain's destruction and concealment of colonial records worldwide', *Journal of Imperial and Commonwealth History*, xlv (2017), 697–719.

[21] See G. McLennan, *Marxism and the Methodologies of History* (London, 1981); P. Claus and J. Marriott, *History: an Introduction to Theory, Method and Practice* (London, 2017);

tended to bristle at the very word. They associated it either with formal sociology or with Teutonic abstraction – or both.

Nowadays, however, both the concept and the word have worked their passage into scholarly usage. It's true that many historians still stick with the more accessible phrase 'research methods'. Yet references to 'methodology' are no longer treated with incomprehension or denial. Instead, just as it's generally agreed that researchers should play fair with their sources, so there's a consensus that they must play fair with their methodologies too. Put simply, how have the data been explored/tested/processed? And are the procedures appropriate? The rise of new digital methods (discussed in detail in chapter 10) is also encouraging researchers to re-examine more traditional approaches and to develop new ones.

Much the commonest approach is for researchers to read/view/listen to many different sources; to evaluate them; to compare and contrast them together; and to use them to construct conclusions, in the context of the secondary literature. That common-sense process is sometimes derided as theoretically 'naive'. Yet it has the great advantage of being robust, explainable and readily communicated to a wider audience. Indeed, history researchers generally do not apply ready-made theories (especially as there are often rival variants); and, if they do follow a particular 'line', then they still have to test it critically too. The crucial feature, in every case, is to explain clearly what approach has been taken and why.

There are also a myriad of technical procedures, designed to enhance the analysis. To take just one example, the process of radiocarbon dating allows researchers to establish the production date of material objects which do not speak for themselves.[22] All well and excellent. But again, readers should be invited to share a rigorous methodology critique, along with the source critique.

In shorthand, the research methods are sometimes divided into a polarity, known respectively as 'soft', meaning qualitative and subjective, and 'hard', meaning quantitative and impersonal.[23] But those terms are unfortunately loaded. 'Soft' techniques may seem too easy and too cosy.

J. W. Moses and T. L. Knutsen (ed.), *Ways of Knowing: Competing Methodologies in Social and Political Research* (London, 2019).

[22] W. Horn, 'The potential and limitations of radiocarbon dating in the Middle Ages: the art historian's view', in *Scientific Methods in Medieval Archaeology*, ed. R. Berger (London, 1970), pp. 23–87.

[23] A distinction first made by the British philosopher Gilbert Ryle (1900–76): see G. Ryle, *On Thinking* (London, 1979). For assessments of 'soft' techniques, see ch. 11.

'Hard' approaches, by contrast, rely upon mathematical/quantitative techniques, also known as 'cliometrics'.[24] Typically, they pose precise questions and seek quantified answers. The side-implication is that such exercises enshrine not just 'rigour' and 'accuracy', but also 'difficulty'. And there is some truth in that last characterization, in that advanced cliometric calculations generally require a degree of technical sophistication which is beyond most historians.[25]

Nonetheless, precise statistics, where available and appropriate, are absolutely invaluable. In economic and demographic history, they usefully reveal both scale and trends – and they can be used to calculate the relationship between different variables, allowing always for the null hypothesis that no meaningful relationship exists.[26] Another new process that is gaining popularity within digital humanities is known as 'distant reading', which entails counting words and their associated meanings. (For more, see chapter 10.)

Yet the conventional 'hard/soft' dichotomy is ultimately misleading in that all historical researchers seek rigour and accuracy. As a result, many practitioners, like most social scientists today, use a mixture of qualitative and quantitative approaches, chosen as relevant to the subject in hand.[27]

What matters, therefore, is the aptness of each approach, whether qualitative, quantitative or mixed. All methods should pass three tests: first, that the sources are good enough to carry the analytical superstructure; second, that the techniques are not time-consuming beyond the remit of the project; and third, that there is no risk of expending time and effort to reveal an answer that was obvious from the start.

Specifically, on that point, it's vital to ensure that no conclusions are inadvertently built into the methodology or the system of data classification. Unchecked assumptions about gender, race and/or class, for example, can produce distortions by inadvertently inserting conventional prejudices into

---

[24] R. Floud, *An Introduction to Quantitative Methods for Historians* (London, 1973, 1979); P. Hudson, *History by Numbers: an Introduction to Quantitative Approaches* (London, 2000); C. Feinstein and M. Thomas, *Making History Count: a Primer in Quantitative Methods for Historians* (Cambridge, 2002).

[25] See further reflections in R. W. Fogel, 'The limits of quantitative methods in history', *American Historical Review*, lxxx (1975), 329–50; J. S. Lyons et al. (ed.), *Reflections on the Cliometrics Revolution: Conversations with Economic Historians* (London, 2008).

[26] Hudson, *History by Numbers*, pp. 53–167.

[27] A. Campbell et al., *Research Design in Social Work: Qualitative, Quantitative and Mixed Methods* (Los Angeles, Calif., 2016).

the organizational categories.[28] Instead, methodologies must enhance, not pre-determine, the analysis.

5.5 Summary: the open-ended quest

Studying history is genuinely fun and incomparably stimulating – and that's what keeps researchers going. Finding, not finding, scrutinizing, assessing, comparing, collating and interpreting evidence from the past can entail hard mental graft, which never seems to end. (The past is infinite.)

Not every project will yield the purest gold. But there is always scope for great discoveries and new interpretations. Or, equally, breakthroughs can be built upon many small steps. In all cases, researchers have to explain themselves to others – and, better still, to convince them. The process should always be dialogic; the quest open-ended.

Seeking fresh knowledge means entering into the unknown. As a quizzical dictum, often attributed to the great exploratory physicist Albert Einstein, mused: 'If we knew what it was we were doing, it would not be called "Research", would it?'.[29]

---

[28] See P. J. Corfield, 'Problems in classifying social class by occupation', in *Elections in Metropolitan London, 1700–1850, Vol. I*, ed. Green, Corfield and Harvey, pp. 441–56.

[29] Quotation commonly ascribed to Albert Einstein, as seemingly reflecting his views, though the attribution remains uncertain: see D. Hirshman, 'Adventures in fact-checking: Einstein quote edition': <https://asociologist.com/2010/09/04/adventures-in-fact-checking-einstein-quote-edition> [accessed 29 April 2021].

6. Managing masses of data

SIGNPOST: Relevant to all researchers

The 'Behemoth' is a terrifyingly powerful mythological beast, signifying primal chaos, from the Biblical Book of Job (40:15–24).

6.1 The flood of information

Gustave Flaubert observed in 1852 that 'Writing history is like drinking an ocean and pissing a cupful'.[1] And he was right. Every big history project is an exercise in controlling a flood of notes and documents. Flaubert, whose evocative novels were steeped in history, knew the struggle to control the

---

[1] Gustave Flaubert (1821–80): 'Il faut boire des océans et les repisser', letter to Louise Colet, 8 May 1852, in G. Flaubert, *Correspondance*, ed. J. Bruneau (Paris, 1972–98), vol. 2, p. 86.

research Behemoth.[2] In a world of foolscap and index cards, organizing the information collected in archives and from secondary reading was an individual choice – sometimes an arcane practice passed down from supervisor to student. In part, too, how notes were organized was driven by the kind of source material that was being consulted.

Famously, historian Keith Thomas created a system of note-taking which entailed writing notes on single sides of sheets of paper, entering the bibliographical details of the core source in his personal index book and then cutting the sheets of paper into fragments, which were then allocated to separate envelopes by theme. When an envelope was full to bursting, it suggested a possible topic for a book or essay.[3] As Thomas's work was chiefly based on the collections of the Bodleian Library, this system worked well for him – and allowed him to develop an unusual writing style that juxtaposed many different quotations from different sources.[4] Other researchers advocate filing notes by subject; or organizing collections of index cards, with keywords.

None of those older systems, however, are fully adequate for modern-day research. With few exceptions, most archives now encourage researchers to take photographs of original documents, while many primary sources are most easily consulted online; and the vast majority of secondary readings, particularly articles, come in the form of PDFs (files in portable document format). In the wake of the Covid-19 pandemic (2020), Britain's National Archives at Kew even stopped researchers from bringing pencil and paper into their search rooms.

All of this makes it much easier to accumulate ever-larger bodies of evidence, but it also poses a real challenge of how to order the flood of notes – and how to find a quotation – among a billion words of source material. Researchers have to update continuously in the new 'digital age'.[5]

---

[2] See the illustration that opens this chapter.

[3] K. Thomas, 'Diary: working methods', *London Review of Books*, xxxii (10 June 2020).

[4] See K. Thomas, *Religion and the Decline of Magic: Studies in Popular Beliefs in Sixteenth-and Seventeenth-Century England* (London, 1971); *Man and the Natural World: Changing Attitudes in England, 1500–1800* (London, 1983); *The Ends of Life: Roads to Fulfilment in Early Modern England* (Oxford, 2009); *In Pursuit of Civility: Manners and Civilization in Early Modern England* (London, 2018).

[5] D. J. Cohen and R. Rosenzweig, *Digital History: a Guide to Gathering, Presenting and Preserving the Past on the Web* (Philadelphia, Pa., 2006); L. Levenberg, T. Neilson and D. Rheams (ed.), *Research Methods for the Digital Humanities* (London, 2018); I. Milligan, *History in the Age of Abundance: How the Web Is Transforming Historical Research* (London, 2019); R. Risam, *New Digital Worlds: Postcolonial Digital Humanities in Theory, Practice*

There are a dozen technical solutions to this problem, and commercial firms eager to sell a data management package. But before committing to any one system, it's best to think hard about both the nature of the sources that are being used and the kind of history that is being written. Some projects will essentially be based on a single source. It is entirely possible to create a doctorate (or book) on the basis of the published *British Parliamentary Papers*, or from a single archive. Alternatively, one project can draw upon a dozen different archives, and a hundred different types of source material.

As a result, the chosen research data management system will need to be keyed to the relevant sources. If working from published material, for example, the precise edition and page references will be important, while if working in an uncatalogued collection (there are a surprising number still to be found), it is necessary to develop a system from scratch to describe how to find a particular item.

The first point to remember is that researchers will eventually have to be able to write footnotes or endnotes which allow others to trace the precise research journey. The choice between footnotes at the foot of the page or endnotes at the end of each chapter (or at the end of the book) is often specified by publishers, journal editors and/or examination regulations. Where authors have a free choice, footnotes are generally recommended for scholarly presentations. But ultimately these things are a matter of choice.

Whatever system is chosen, it's vital to ensure that it will record all the information needed for a citation. Some scholarly websites give helpful pointers as to how each individual document is to be cited.[6] But not all do so. Researchers must therefore check in every case. If the archival reference is not associated with the correct document title and folio references, for instance, and that reference is then demanded for the final doctoral thesis, researchers will find themselves undertaking days of unnecessary (and frankly boring) labour to recover the missing information.

A second point for researchers then follows: *can you find it?* It is remarkable how quickly even key details can be forgotten! And coming back to a file of a thousand pages in search of a single quotation is daunting, even assuming that it's possible to conduct a keyword search. Hence it's vital for

---

and Pedagogy (Evanston, Ill., 2019); H. Salmi, *What Is Digital History?* (Cambridge, 2020); and A. Crymble, *Technology and the Historian: Transformations in the Digital Age* (Urbana, Ill., 2021).

[6] See, eg, the *Old Bailey Proceedings Online*: <https://www.oldbaileyonline.org/index .jsp> [accessed 24 January 2022].

all researchers to find some way of 'indexing', or keywording, or tagging the research notes and images.

And a third point: *are the notes easy to use when writing?* People write differently, but history is always a confection of comment and evidence; and organizing the evidence and ensuring that every quotation is accurate, and every statistic is correct, is key. In other words, researchers should work out how they write and use evidence – and organize references accordingly. And it's worth adding here that there are two common styles of presenting notes (as well as many variations). The Harvard system locates all bibliographical details of sources at the end of a given piece of work, and cites within the text (in brackets) simply the author surname, date of publication and page references, if needed. It works flexibly and well when citing single published works, but is cumbersome for referencing many sources, and especially for citing non-published sources (documents; art objects; artefacts), which often have lengthy call-marks.

By contrast, the Oxford system (used in this *Guide*) inserts superscripts in the text at key junctures, and then places all bibliographical information in a running sequence of footnotes or endnotes. These also allow scope for additional commentary from authors, although these days pithiness is in vogue. Either way, readers should be able to track all key sources, whether primary or secondary. Of course, they don't all do so. But examiners will do – and the option should be open to all comers.[7]

6.2 Identifying files: what's in a name?

Any long-form piece of history-writing will be based on dozens or hundreds of separate files. Many will be PDFs, but others will be images of original documents; or data might be recorded in spreadsheets and CSV (comma-separated values) files. Or 3D models, maps and KMZ files might be used; or XML, audio and video files. To keep track of all these files, a consistent and 'human-readable' system of file names is essential. Most people create a new hierarchical system of folders (backed up to the cloud) that reflects the topics in a bigger project. But an alternative system is to organize by archive or source type. The important thing is that the chosen file names are human readable, clear and distinctive. A file called chapter 2, which holds automatically generated file names – a string of numbers and letters – will be impossible to manage when it comes to organizing research materials.

---

[7] Grafton, *The Footnote*; F. A. Burkle-Young and S. R. Maley, *The Art of the Footnote: the Intelligent Student's Guide to the Art and Science of Annotating Texts* (London, 1996).

In contrast, a file, perhaps called 'historiography, chapter 2', that includes short, readable versions of the titles of individual items – such as Beattie, *English Detectives*, 2012.pdf[8] – is going to be much more helpful. Keywords can also be added to file names – though adding more than two or three is likely to become unwieldy.

Archival photographs are particularly difficult to organize effectively. There are new(ish) systems that allow researchers to rename and organize photographs directly from phone or camera. The leading system for historians at the moment is *Tropy*.[9] It's a system which allows an archival reference and keywords to be used, so that images are automatically renamed. That process makes managing and sharing such images much easier.

However, even without using an image management system, it is important to ensure that absolutely all the information needed to cite a page of photographed manuscript is included. It is worth, for example, creating a separate folder for all the images of a single document, and using the archival reference and title as the folder name. It is also important that the first image taken in a series of images is of the spine, cover or first page of a document, and includes the archival reference.

Equally challenging are online sources. Simply recording a URL (Uniform Resource Locator, or web address) is not good enough. Many sites change and evolve, and the information found one month could well be gone the next. A lot of sites also insist on registering or signing in (or using library sign-in systems like Shiboleth or OpenAthens). This method creates a session URL, but, unfortunately, it can't be shared with other researchers and won't work at a later date.[10]

Most websites that allow keyword searching also create a 'search URL', which includes all the information in a search form. But these URLs quickly become both unreadable and fragile. Many sites will allow researchers to copy or download specific items and objects, and this technique offers one solution. Renaming the files will then help to organize them.

Another solution is to use the Wayback Machine and Internet Archive. This method allows users to 'archive' a specific website, as it appears on the day it was consulted. The new URL can then be saved, allowing researchers to be certain of finding (and being able to cite) the original page, as it

---

[8] Indicating J. M. Beattie, *The First English Detectives: the Bow Street Runners and the Policing of London, 1750–1840* (London, 2012).

[9] <https://tropy.org> [accessed 30 April 2021].

[10] For a detailed discussion of these issues, see T. Hitchcock, 'Judging a book by its URLs', <http://historyonics.blogspot.com/search/label/URL> [accessed 22 Dec. 2020].

was when *originally* consulted. The Wayback Machine is the closest thing available to an 'archive' of the internet.[11]

6.3 Using data management tools: do I, or don't I?

There are innumerable data management tools out there that are worth considering. Endnote[12] and Envivo[13] are two of the most popular commercial packages. However, they cost money – and once researchers start using a package, they may find that they are caught in a system that runs into trouble. Software companies go bust; packages stop being supported; and apparently secure data is suddenly impossible to access. Most packages will allow the export of data to other systems, but before committing to any single package, it's crucial to ensure that escape can be made, if need be, with all data intact.

The advantages with data management tools can be huge, and many historians swear by them. They allow clear labelling of all items, matched with the capacity to organize them and insert relevant keywords. They also facilitate complex searches and come with a range of in-built tools – for visualizing and analysing the mass of notes. Most usefully of all, most data management systems will allow the creation of automatic links to Word documents, enabling the generation of footnotes and citations directly from stored research materials.

Several alternatives are free to users. The most popular is Zotero.[14] This service was created by the Center for History and New Media at George Mason University, Virginia, USA; and it is one of a series of tools, including Omeka and Tropy, which are designed specifically for historians and to aid historical research. Zotero allows users to create a free account, and either to develop their own bibliography or to share themed bibliographies created by others. It also allows users to upload PDFs to their accounts, and then to search them; and to relate these items to the full text in Google Books.

What's more, through a series of plug-ins, researchers can then automatically generate an accurate record of every item read elsewhere. When reading an article online, a simple click of the mouse will generate a full citation and copy the item to each individual's Zotero account. Later, selected items, or indeed the whole bibliography, can be exported to whatever format is

---

[11] Created 24 Oct. 2001 by a non-profit organization in San Francisco: see <https://archive.org/web> [accessed 29 April 2021].

[12] <https://access.clarivate.com/login?app=endnote> [accessed 29 April 2021].

[13] <https://enviosystems.com> [accessed 29 April 2021].

[14] For Zotero, 'Your Personal Research Assistant', see <https://www.zotero.org> [accessed 29 April 2021].

needed. And when writing, a plug-in for Word allows researchers to create a footnote – or an in-line citation – by entering the first few letters of an author's name or item title.

In sum, Zotero is not a comprehensive data management system, but it reproduces many of the functions of expensive commercial packages, and in combination with a well-structured hierarchy of computer files, it makes for a good compromise.

6.4 Finding shorter shortcuts

Once research materials have been assembled, there are also numerous tools available to help in the process of interrogating and understanding them.[15] The tools mentioned below are some of the more popular ones at the time of writing, but new ones emerge regularly, and old ones fall out of fashion.

When working with large amounts of plain text, there are a series of approaches drawn from Corpus Linguistics,[16] which historians are increasingly using. These allow the study of word frequency and context, and they rapidly identify and assess relevant phrases from a large 'corpus' or set of texts. The most popular currently is Voyant Tools,[17] which enables users to upload text and analyse it in real time.

In one pioneering example of systematic data searching, the Japanese social historian Kazuhiko Kondo combed through thousands of eighteenth-century publications. He used a combination of digitized resources including EEBO (Early English Books Online),[18] ECCO (Eighteenth-Century Collections Online)[19] and MOMW (the digital economics library entitled Making of the Modern World).[20] He was seeking to test a specific query, in two parts. Was the phrase 'moral economy' used in publications

---

[15] For the importance of clarifying methodologies and sampling systems, see K. H. Leetaru, *Data Mining Methods for the Content Analyst: an Introduction to the Computational Analysis of Content* (New York, 2012); G. Schiuma and D. Carlucci, *Big Data in the Arts and Humanities: Theory and Practice* (Boca Raton, Fla., 2018); K. Leetaru, 'Big data revolutions will be sampled: how "big data" has come to mean "small sampled data"', *Forbes Magazine*, 17 Feb. 2019: <https://www.forbes.com/sites/kalevleetaru/2019/02/17/the-big-data-revolution-will-be-sampled-how-big-data-has-come-to-mean-small-sampled-data/#27f3e310199e> [accessed 29 April 2021].

[16] Corpus Linguistics is defined as the study of linguistics based upon analysis of 'real-world' texts in their authentic state.

[17] Voyant, 'See through your text': <https://voyant-tools.org> [accessed 29 April 2021].

[18] <https://eebo.chadwyck.com/home>, moved to new proQuest website in late August 2019: <https://www.proquest.com> [accessed 29 April 2021].

[19] <https://quod.lib.umich.edu/e/ecco> [accessed 29 April 2021].

[20] Making of the Modern World is an online collection, based upon the Goldsmiths'-Kress Library of Economic Literature, 1450–1850, expanded to include many other economic

during this period? (*Answer: Yes.*) And did it have the polemical meaning attributed to it by the British Marxist historian E. P. Thompson? (*Answer: Yes, but only partially.*)[21] Kondo's findings thus helpfully illuminated a rumbling historical debate. Some eighteenth-century commentators (but definitely not all) did indeed appeal to a 'moral' alternative to what they denounced as a worldly and amoral 'political economy'.

Different researchers choose different combinations of search method-ologies, as suitable for each specific task. Overall, meanwhile, it's a reasonable prediction that Corpus Linguistics will continue to gain in relevance and popularity – and that the technical speed and sophistication of such approaches will continue to grow.

For all those working with structured data – in the form of spreadsheets or as CSV files, or in a database – there are tools like OpenRefine.[22] These tools allow researchers to re-organize and analyse their data with great rapidity. And the power of spreadsheet packages like Excel, for the analysis and translation of data, should not be underestimated. Between macros and plug-ins, Word and other word-processing software can also act as powerful text management systems.

Jupyter Notebooks[23] are also increasingly being advocated as a way of managing the analysis of research materials. These allow researchers to incorporate data, along with elements of computer code, both to develop and to clean research material; and to run more complex processes, without researchers having to write code themselves. When working with large bodies of structured data, such systems are worth the effort of learning how to use them.

But even for those who aren't comfortable with complex online and computer-based systems, there are still a lot of small 'cheats' that will make writing history easier. Simply using control-F in a browser will save readers from monotonous skim-reading when searching through a large text; and many bibliographies support automated citation services. The Bibliography

---

documents to 1945: see <https://www.gale.com/intl/primary-sources/the-making-of-the-modern-world> [accessed 29 April 2021].

[21] See both K. Kondo, '"Moral Economy" retried in the digital archives', *Bulletin of the Graduate School of Humanities & Sociology, Rissho University [Japan]*, xxxv (March 2019), 21–36; and original essay by E. P. Thompson, 'The moral economy of the English crowd in the eighteenth century' (London, 1971), repr. in E. P. Thompson, *Customs in Common* (London, 1991), pp. 185–258.

[22] OpenRefine offers itself as 'a powerful tool for working with messy data': <https://openrefine.org> [accessed 29 April 2021].

[23] <https://jupyter.org> [accessed 29 April 2021].

of British and Irish History (BBIH), for instance – a key research tool for all working in the areas of British and Irish history[24] – allows users to right-click on any item and generate a citation in any of the most common formats, which in turn can be cut and pasted into a footnote. One of the nice things about working on larger projects is that it is worth the time spent learning new packages, and new tricks. And that's precisely because researchers are then investing two or three or more years in getting it right.

6.5 Summary: losing data – and finding it again

At some point, historians find themselves staring at a computer screen, and the perfect quotation to support a complex argument will rise to mind. Memory insists that it's been read somewhere significant. It was on the upper-left-hand side of the screen – or perhaps it was in a large green book, about two-thirds of the way through – but certainly somewhere. Many a long afternoon can be spent trying to locate the quotation. And, when it's found, it often turns out not to be as perfect as was imperfectly remembered.

Good data management allows researchers to organize their thoughts as they proceed, as well as to organize their writing; and, above all, to think more critically about what the project is actually trying to achieve. With the right tools, researching and writing becomes infinitely more efficient, and infinitely more fun.

Overall, the system chosen by each researcher does not need to be complex, or technically challenging. It just needs to be suitable for the task in hand – and it will keep those wasted afternoons, looking for that perfect quotation, down to a minimum.

[24] Hosted by University of London's Institute of Historical Research: <https://www.his tory.ac.uk/publications/bibliography-british-and-irish-history> [accessed 29 April 2021].

PART II
Writing, analysing, interpreting

7. Writing as a historian

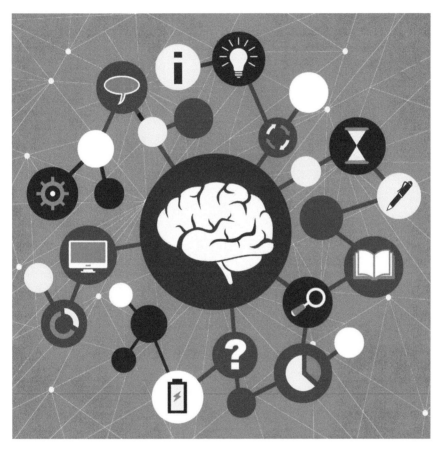

Historian's mind-map.

7.1 The bedrock – learning to enjoy

Writing is a craft skill, which can be improved with practice – lots of practice. So it is crucial to enjoy the art of communication and to take pleasure in the journey. Academic prose should not be too chatty but neither should it be dull. Between these extremes, there is ample scope to find a personal voice and to develop a distinctive style. After all, the great advantage of being oneself on the page is that no-one else can do the job so well.

In practice, the styles of history-writing can be hugely varied; and a good thing too. It's a remarkably capacious genre: from high theory and meta-narratives, through to micro-histories and biography. Other people's experiences and advice provide a useful starting-point, as summarized in many fine guides.[1] It's also worth identifying impressive authors and then working out which elements of their prose style contribute to the impressive effect. But there are no formal rules.

For a start, it's good not to be bored, since bored writers tend to write boring prose; and it's even better to convey enthusiasm, without being too gushing. Historians characteristically need to command both big issues and much small detail. So it's helpful to have some imagined readers in mind, and ask yourself: will this account make sense to them? It's not possible to make every point instantly. Instead, it's essential to consider carefully how arguments should be made, in what sequence, and with what evidence. And then to signal clearly how the intellectual journey will unfold. Readers who are forewarned will be far more receptive to the arguments.

One central, if negative, point should not need labouring. That is: writers should never plagiarize, which means using other people's unchanged words without acknowledgement.[2] If writing that 'Experience is the name everyone gives to their mistakes', the statement should be shown in quotation marks, with a note to explain that it comes from Oscar Wilde's play *Lady Windermere's Fan* (1892).[3] Failure to acknowledge direct borrowing is intellectual theft. It's seriously bad faith, and is not forgiven. There have been cases of history students falsifying their dissertations by plagiarizing the words of published authors. One tiny slip may arguably be pardoned as a genuine mistake, from which experience can be gained. Yet anything more systematic means that the entire piece of work is failed outright.

Plagiarists are not only trying to cheat the educational system; they are also cheating themselves. They are spending time and money on the outer shell of learning, without gaining any worthwhile inner reality.

[1] J. Bolker, *Writing Your Dissertation in Fifteen Minutes a Day: a Guide to Starting, Revising and Finishing Your Doctoral Thesis* (New York, 1998); M. E. Page and R. A. Marius, *A Short Guide to Writing about History* (Harlow, 2014); A. Brundage, *Going to the Sources: a Guide to Historical Research and Writing* (Hoboken, N.J., 2018).

[2] For a legal expert's critique of examples in literature, art, film, music and academic life, see R. A. Posner, *The Little Book of Plagiarism* (New York, 2007).

[3] O. Wilde, *Lady Windermere's Fan* (London, 1892), in *The Complete Works*, ed. V. Holland (London, 1968), p. 418: spoken by Mr Dumby in Act 3.

Furthermore, they are likely to be detected in these days of techno-assisted checking – thus losing their good reputations for no purpose. Similarly, published authors who plagiarize are sailing under false colours – ultimately leading to their own detriment as well as deceiving sincere readers who expect better. But enough of negatives! Completing a big, original project offers an ideal opportunity for learning to enjoy writing and finding a personal voice.

7.2 Mind-mapping

A starting technique which suits many (but not all) is the exercise of mind-mapping. It's an easy visual method of experimenting with plans for a given project. After an initial brainstorming exercise, all the main themes and sources are jotted down as key points, randomly distributed on a big blank page. Then multiple linkage lines can be drawn between them, as shown in the illustration that opens this chapter. And the maps can be scribbled and re-scribbled again and again. It's a way of reviewing many variants of the intellectual terrain.[4]

Lateral thinking opens up new vistas. Then, after a while, the mind-map can be used as the basis from which a traditional linear plan can be devised. It should contain a list of chapter headings, with a broad indication of their contents. But nothing should be viewed as set in stone, since all plans are liable to be adapted as the research and writing unfolds. Some people don't appreciate or gain from such visualizations. While one of the authors of this book employs mind-mapping for planning big projects (PJC), the other actively dislikes the technique (TH). So for those who don't appreciate visualizations, it's enough to start with a draft linear plan – written, revised, rewritten and revised again – running from point 1 (introduction) through to the final conclusion.

Another style of preparation is to start by reviewing the evidence and the secondary literature, essentially ordering the sequence of data (and footnotes) before settling down to write the prose. This approach has two advantages. It guarantees that the evidence governs the overall argument. And it also ensures that unsupported hyperbole is kept to a minimum. Again, however, this method is not for everyone, as some prefer to work out the overall argument as they write, rather than at the very start.

Generally, the key point is that history-writing does not lend itself to exposition by free-association and stream-of-consciousness. So there must

---

[4] Among many guides, see T. Buzan, *Mind-Mapping* (Harlow, 2006).

be some coherent preliminary planning. One practical point is worth noting here: in general, over-long chapters (more than 7,500–8,000 words) should appear only sparingly, if at all. Again, however, there's no absolute rule. All depends on context and the best way of making the case.

Then it's vital to start with some preliminary definitions of the field. The first steps in the long journey need particularly clear signalling. However, there are often so many terms and concepts to confront that it's not necessary to deal with everything at once. A torrent of instant explanations can be overwhelming. Instead, definitions can be spread throughout the text, as needed. Whenever they do appear, they should be explained clearly and used consistently. Readers are rightly annoyed if the terms of debate are covertly changed mid-course. And if a coherent analytical thread is lost, the project dissolves back into details, which alone don't make a case.

During the writing process, by the way, it's perfectly normal for definitions to be adapted and revised. But the crucial point is that, at the end, they should be standardized and rendered consistent throughout. The intellectual journey commonly entails revision and reconsideration along the route – but, finally, it needs to be presented with a coherent plan *and* clear way-markers.

7.3 Writing and annotating throughout

Researchers should write constantly, as explained earlier (section 3.4). It goes without saying that copies of the latest draft chapters and notes should always be kept safely. It's also vital that filing systems ensure accurate 'version control', either by naming files clearly or by moving earlier drafts into separate folders. Otherwise it's fatally easy to get confused between conflicting texts.

Once draft chapters are getting close to completion, it's good practice to print them out in their entirety and to read them through, away from the computer. Some people even like to speak the whole text aloud – perhaps to an attentive audience of cat or dog. It's certainly much easier to spot flaws when away from the screen. Otherwise, familiarity leads authors to develop blind spots for typos, errors and verbal tics.

History-writing then entails much polishing and editing. Often, first drafts are too wordy and gain from being firmly cut.[5] Another element of good practice is to get a frank friend (as well as the supervisor) to give a critical reading. But the chosen person needs to hit the happy medium between complete adulation (useless) and complete vituperation (demotivating). In

---

[5] Editorial control generates the evocative detective story by C. McCabe, *The Face on the Cutting-Room Floor* (London, 1937, 1986), p. 15: 'You have to re-edit the junk'.

exchange, it's comradely to return the service. Indeed, providing a friend with a fair critique is an invaluable skill.

Of course, all serious academic analysis (except for textbooks and some overview essays) needs the support of evidence. So the slog of annotation, whether in footnotes or endnotes, should be done concurrently – or close to concurrently – as the writing unfolds. In practice, fluent composition often runs a few paragraphs ahead of the laborious process of documentation. That's fine, to keep the prose flowing. On the other hand, it's crucial not to write too far ahead of completing the notes. Otherwise hours of merry writing will turn out to need complete revision, once the detailed facts, quotations, references and so forth are checked and inserted.

These days, online resources enable notes to be generated automatically and in the correct format as the writing progresses, thus keeping the whole process in synchronization (as explained in chapter 6). But – whether with or without technical aids – a serious historical study is not fully finished unless and until it's fully documented.[6] And, even so, it's an annoying feature of life that some small error is likely to have slipped under the radar (!): meaning that authors need to stay constantly vigilant.

7.4 Incorporating variety/light and shade

As a discipline, history has a strong track record of presenting complexity in accessible styles, even if, admittedly, not all practitioners live up to the ideal. So there's a standing invitation to avoid monotony and incorporate variety. Historical studies are not the same as fiction, but many eloquent works of history do make admirable contributions to literature.[7] Part of the impact of E. P. Thompson's much-debated study of *The Making of the English Working Class* (1963 and still in print) stems from his impassioned and luxuriant prose style.[8] It's therefore good practice from the start (as already emphasized) to think creatively about the art of writing. And, having thought, then to hone a personal style.

Illustrations may well be integral to the discussion; but, even if not, their addition is very helpful in catching the reader's attention. The same applies

---

[6] Discussed fully in sect. 6.1.

[7] For relevant discussions, see A. Curthoys and J. Docker, *Is History Fiction?* (Sydney, 2006); A Curthoys and A. McGrath, *How to Write the History That People Want to Read* (Basingstoke, 2011).

[8] See E. P. Thompson, *Making of the English Working Class*, and A. Curthoys, 'History as a form of literature: E. P. Thompson's *The Making of the English Working Class*', in *TEXT Special Issue 28: Fictional Histories and Historical Fiction – Writing History in the Twenty-First Century*, ed. C. Nelson and C. de Matos (April 2015), pp. 1–14.

to maps, graphs, tables and all other forms of visual exposition.[9] All these are admirable elements of the communications repertoire. At the same time, it's stimulating to write with a good range of vocabulary and phrasing. And it's also a pleasant challenge, should the need arise, to invent new words[10] – provided that they make a genuine contribution to the debate.

Careful attention should also be paid to the length of both sentences and paragraphs. Varying these can add momentum. Text that is written throughout in long sentences, in densely Latinate terminology, is often hard to follow. Yet the other extreme has problems too. Text that proceeds by non-stop, rat-a-tat, terse, sub-Hemingwayian sentences, all studded with short, punchy Anglo-Saxon nouns, can start by being stimulating and then become numbing.

Variation is the key:

Here now, to take but one example, this considered statement is expounded with careful, even studied, deliberation, in order to emphasize a basic element of human understanding – so crucial to a globally dispersed and migratory species – which learns not only through the repeated, quick assimilation of many diverse nuggets of immediate information but equally through processes of deep pondering and prolonged slow fixation upon big substantive problems, whether close at hand or posing long-term opportunities/threats. (75 words)

Meanwhile, brevity can punch home a message:

Humans characteristically combine quick assimilation with deep thought. (8 words)

Both sentences make a considered statement of the same point, but the first version is virtually unreadable, while the brevity of the second may conceal its full significance. One self-monitoring strategy is for authors to upload their draft chapters onto online facilities, like Voyant Tools (discussed in chapter 6). This mechanism will provide textual statistics, including details of average sentence length; the range of vocabulary employed; and, if relevant, the overuse of pet phrases. Such stringent methods are not to everyone's taste, but authors should find some means of self-checking to help their eventual readers.

---

[9] K. Hentschel, *Mapping the Spectrum: Techniques of Visual Representation in Research and Teaching* (Oxford, 2002).

[10] J. Green, *New Words: a Dictionary of Neologisms since 1960* (London, 1991); E. Mattiello, *Analogy in Word-Formation: a Study in English Neologisms and Occasionalisms* (Berlin, 2017).

7.5 *Knowing and refuting the contrary arguments*

Advocacy works best not by caricaturing opposite views but by understanding them, in order to refute them successfully.[11] The best courtroom lawyers and politicians are well aware of this rule. There's no point in pouring scorn upon a caricature of a 'straw man', since its defeat leaves untouched those who believe in the alternative version that stands behind it. Thus the best way to refute an argument, if refutation is required, is to know it really well and then to point out its weakest points, while countering its strongest ones.

Learning to debate, fairly but firmly, is an essential art for history researchers. It entails both making positive points for a case *and* being able to refute critical objections to that case. Researchers are not exactly like courtroom lawyers, who are paid to take one side or another, whatever their private beliefs in the guilt or innocence of the defendant. Historians usually believe firmly in both their evidence and their arguments. Yet it's still helpful to know how best to advance a case – and to defend it against criticism.

Techniques of argument can be honed by regular participation in academic seminars (see chapter 14). And mental agility can be developed by debating with oneself. From time to time, it's salutary to look at the evidence assembled and to ask: *'Have I got things completely wrong?' 'What other ways are there of interpreting this material?'* Indeed, it's quite normal for historians to experience moments when they simultaneously hold three different views about an event or issue. Constantly reviewing the argumentative options as impartially as possible is the best way to test the strengths and weaknesses of an approach – and eventually to decide one's own view.

When writing, it's necessary from time to time to indicate one's stance on disputed points. That is again best done courteously but firmly. However, it's unwise to get stuck in just one controversy. Providing an all-out attack on a rival interpretation will attract immediate attention. But debates change over time. It's not advisable to become known simply as the intellectual slayer of X, when in a decade's time X might be completely forgotten, partly through the efforts of the critics who have cut him or her down to size. Cogent criticisms should therefore be blended with offering positive alternatives. In many respects, 'good', well-informed history drives out 'bad' work, which means that making a strong, positive intervention is a better way of changing the field than launching into vociferous attack.

---

[11] R. DuCann, *The Art of the Advocate* (London, 1993); B. Brunwin and M. Smith, *'Making Your Case': a Process for Developing the Language of Argument and Persuasion* (Howden, 2004).

Pure negativism dies quickly. Successful refutation, well supported with evidence, can, meanwhile, win an argument. Historical debates rarely stop absolutely dead in their tracks, just like that. Yet arguments are won or lost. Knowledge progresses. So, to take an already cited factual example, historians no longer assert that there were popular riots in England in 1752 over the issue of calendar reform. Why not? Because it has been shown conclusively (as noted previously in section 5.2) that no such riots occurred.

7.6 Developing a message

Every piece of writing needs an argument or core message. Otherwise, the effort won't be worthwhile. Yet the full interlocking details of the message will emerge only in the course of writing. So researchers often begin with working titles for chapters and sub-sections, and then finalize them about three-quarters of the way through the writing process. Unfolding a message throughout a big project is a fine art. If things are too clear-cut and fixed at the very start, then there's no scope for growth and development.

On the other hand, if the discussion is too nebulous at the start, it may well remain nebulous throughout. The message emerges as ideas are tested against evidence, and vice versa. By the end, the researcher should know where the journey has led – and can tell the world. It may also mean going back to the start to revise for consistency, as already advised when talking of definitions.

Far from every historical study will lead to conclusions of cosmic significance. It's perfectly valid and important to have results which are local and contingent. So the requirement to put a study into its wider context is certainly not a call for the sudden insertion of a grand theory. Historians don't have to sign up to any single ideology or faith or worldview. Some do write with one big concept or interpretation in mind, organizing their material accordingly; and it is impossible to escape entirely the insistent present and its present-mindedness. Still, many historians take a distinctly eclectic approach, collecting and probing masses of diverse data.

Nonetheless, it is deeply disappointing if, after a big research project, no assessment of its wider importance is offered. What big picture has been illuminated? Or should a big interpretation be amended? Or be challenged outright? Does a specific case fit into any long-term trend? Or does it subvert such a postulated trend and suggest an alternative? Or was it a complete exception to prove the rule? And so forth.

Answers may be couched as interim or provisional assessments. But, after years of study, researchers are experts in their fields; and people want to hear their conclusions. By way of summary, it is becoming increasingly common for authors to be asked, whether by supervisors, journal editors or seminar organizers, to write a short abstract (say, 200 words) of their arguments. It's an invaluable discipline, extracting, from a mass of details, the message.

7.7 Summary: ending strongly

Endings should therefore be conveyed strongly, even if the topic is a sad one and the conclusion is pessimistic. Just to clarify, this advice does not propose that all final words must contain nothing but pollyanna-happiness. But it means that endings should not be so evasive or so bland that in effect they say nothing.

It's equally dispiriting for a research study to end with nothing other than a call for more research. That conclusion is not only lazy; it is also self-undermining. If the research done to date is so feeble that no conclusions can be drawn, then why bother to complete it at all?

What then? Much the best recommendation is to draw all the threads together emphatically. The message may be upbeat or downbeat or somewhere in between. It may be expressed as a snappy dictum or, alternatively, as a longer magisterial statement. Yet the outcome should be strongly expressed. Readers as well as authors have been on a journey and they want to know where they have arrived. Conclusions matter immensely. The better they encapsulate each historian's mix of evidence and arguments, the better they nail the case.

7.8 Coda: historians' writing spaces and writing rituals

Historical studies are big, complex and slow to write. They cannot be scribbled hastily in a coffee bar or on a train. So it's fruitful to think carefully about a suitable writing space, where it is no penance to spend a lot of time – and where there is space for reference books, personal notes and sundry drafts.

Obvious things help: finding a suitable desk with a comfortable chair in a quiet working area at home or in a library. Or, ideally (shades of Virginia Woolf), setting aside an agreeable workroom at home.[12] Historians without access to such resources, who write on a table at home after the family has gone to bed, should place the table in a quiet location that helps to provide focus. The workstation should be as conducive to mental and physical health as possible – bearing in mind too that some authors prefer to write

---

[12] See inevitably V. Woolf, *A Room of One's Own: an Essay on Women in Relation to Literature* (London, 1929).

while standing.[13] In all cases, good lighting that shines a concentrated pool of light on the working area is invaluable. And some writers also find that ear-plugs or a good set of sound-excluding headphones help to foster a cocoon of heightened concentration.

Other practical tips are worth noting briefly. It's essential from the start to institute good filing and storage arrangements for notes, drafts and supporting documentation, as already noted in chapter 6. Regular removal of clutter and debris is also good practice. Meanwhile, it's essential to keep track of all proposed illustrations, which can be hard to find a second time round. And of course it's vital to back up unfailingly after every batch of writing. The first disastrous time when a big footnoted research chapter, representing months of work, mysteriously 'goes missing' without a back-up should be the last. Today's cloud-based facilities should avert such old-style disasters; but even new-style technology can develop gremlins. Authors: remain vigilant!

Productivity is greatly improved, finally, if researchers can find a good, unbroken span of time for writing, without distractions from phone calls, text messages, emails or any other medium of communication. Many find that at least two 'clear' hours constitute the minimum to get into the zone of creativity. Some authors also follow a specific start-ritual, to signal that their writing time has arrived – and that interruptions are to be discouraged.

People have invented many variants. For instance, the prolific Charles Dickens liked to patrol his house, checking that everything was in order; and he insisted that his writing room be kept completely quiet, with an extra door as a noise baffle. He then arranged nine specific objects in their set positions on his desk, before picking up his pen.[14] These days, many use the sequenced processes of activating computers as their personal starting signal. It's enough to have a known routine and to stick with it. Clearing the decks, getting everything ready – and then a complete focus upon writing – is an invitation to unleash the creative intellect.

---

[13] K. Bowman, *Don't Just Sit There: Transitioning to a Standing and Dynamic Workstation for Whole-Body Health* (Chichester, 2015).

[14] 'What would Dickens do? The rituals and routines of famous writers', The Writers Domain (June 2016): <http://blog.writersdomain.net/what-would-dickens-do-the-rituals-and-routines-of-famous-writers> [accessed 29 April 2021]. See also M. Currey, *Daily Rituals: How Great Minds Make Time, Find Inspiration and Get to Work* (London, 2013); M. Currey, *Daily Rituals: Women at Work* (London, 2019).

8. Doing it in public: historians and social media

Social media now adds a new dimension.

8.1 The new media dimension

In the last twenty years, a whole new component has been added to the process of becoming a historian. It is not formally part of getting a degree; nor does it figure in the criteria used to assess candidates for jobs. Yet it is frequently where doctoral students start to build a reputation, and where they construct a community of fellow travellers. As a result, using social media well is now almost as central to the historical conversation as are seminar presentations, conference attendance and formal peer-reviewed publications. Getting these things right is therefore important.[1]

---

[1] A. Briggs and P. Burke, *A Social History of the Media: From Gutenberg to the Internet* (Cambridge, 2002); J. Van Diyck, *The Culture of Connectivity: a Critical History of Social Media* (Oxford, 2013).

Blogging, Twitter, Facebook, Instagram, TikTok and all their many imitators can be a joyous free-for-all; a democratic space where all voices are heard. At first sight, many of these platforms appear to undercut the gatekeepers of the academy and to create space for new and different voices. They are potentially liberating – and to be applauded, not avoided.

Yet all social media can simultaneously be a poisonous snake-pit of bitter recrimination, of brutal pile-ons and of gross insults. Their very democratic character means that they provide space for racists, homophobes and misogynists; for conspiracy theorists and ethnic nationalists; and just seriously unpleasant people. To participate in these venues can sometimes require a strong stomach. At the same time, there is nothing quite like the sense of community that can be found online, or the expertise accessible through the generosity of '#Twitterstorians'. As important, sometimes humans just enjoy receiving a few cute pictures of pets, or, when feeling down, getting the immediate validation of a cheery 'like' or two in response to a Tweet.

8.2 Self-knowledge: who are you?

The first challenge is creating a professional version of oneself online. There is every possibility that researchers already have four or five social media accounts – some long abandoned, and others used daily to keep in touch with friends. As a result, it's necessary to decide whether to build a 'historian's' presence by adapting those accounts, or by creating new ones. This choice is really down to how much each individual wants to have a personal media identity which is separate from the one shared with a professional community. It may seem a waste to abandon a community of followers just because the username chosen five years ago is irrelevant or embarrassing; or it may be time to update.

Fashions in naming conventions and the use of online anonymity change rapidly. But it's a worthwhile general rule for researchers, when creating a new profile online as a historian, to use their given names in full. A cute nickname dates quickly, and may anyway confuse people when meeting in the flesh. And, while anonymity gives more freedom to say contentious things, historians tend to be serious people. The academic community expects all individuals to own and to defend their opinions.

It is also sensible to choose background images and blog names carefully. A thematic image reflecting a thesis topic or area of study helps ensure that casual visitors get the message. A great image will attract more users. Issues of copyright at this stage should not cause too much concern. A detail from a larger image will normally fall under fair use – and, in the event of an objection, the image can always be removed. It is also sensible to take care when providing a self-description and personal profile. If some casual interest is listed before the core research theme, there's a serious risk of failing to engage with the very people who should be most interested – and interesting as respondents.

8.3 Following others: who are they?

Who to follow is then the next big choice. #Twitterstorians has been an active hashtag on Twitter and Instagram since 2007, when Katrina Gulliver[2] first used it to identify historically relevant Tweets. And in 2015 Jason Kelly compiled a list of all 'Twitterstorians', with analytics of their interactions.[3]

One strategy for building an online community is simply to start following #Twitterstorians. But it's equally powerful to start locally. It's good to follow people in the same department or faculty; to follow other doctoral students; to follow the author of the book you read most recently (if it was any good). And it's as important to stop following people who post things that are not relevant. Time and energy are limited. Spending too much of both online, on social media, just means there is less time for research and face-to-face discussion.

Most history conferences and many seminars have a hashtag. And it has now become commonplace at conferences for a separate discussion and debate to take place on Twitter during the course of the conference – with comments on papers and panels being shared both among the participants on the ground and with a wider global audience. It is worth following these #hashtags as a way of identifying people with similar interests, and those working in similar areas. It's a direct and easy way to participate. It also provides a good opening when meeting people in the flesh – their latest Tweet will serve as a ready-made opening for discussion.

Dan Cohen, the historian of science, once said of Twitter that he enjoyed it mainly because at the end of every week he would know what new articles were published; who had said what; and which conferences he should have attended. For many people, Twitter and other social media act as a filter, allowing them to choose which voices to let through the cacophony. Following the right people, whether a few hundred or several

---

[2] See Katrina Gulliver, historian, writer and academic: @katrinagulliver.

[3] See <https://www.jasonmkelly.com/jason-m-kelly/2015/09/17/twitterstorians-a-list> [accessed 30 April 2021]. For Jason M. Kelly, historian, teacher and engaged citizen, see @Jason_M_Kelly.

thousand, allows researchers to join networks of scholars who work in relevant fields. But one obvious warning applies. Using social media can be addictive; and it's vital not to let media participation crowd out time for everything else.

8.4 Participating: what to say?

Having set up an account, created a profile and decided who to follow, it is time to start using the media to promote one's own work – and to join the debates. It is okay – indeed sensible – to watch quietly for a while, but eventually it's good to start contributing. When doing so, it is vital to remember that everything posted is a public statement and a form of publication.

In formal, peer-reviewed publications, there are reviewers, editors and friends to stop authors from being stupid. Even in the case of a seminar presentation, speakers have time to think about their contributions, and ideally, their supervisors will have read a draft. Online, none of these 'hold-me-back' mechanisms exist. It's fatally easy to over-react, making ill-judged, ill-informed or unintentionally insulting comments. And these dicta will remain in the ether forever. It is thus essential not to respond instantly. Everyone needs a few moments to assess how a comment or a post is likely to be received.

This counsel is not one of timidity. For all with strong perspectives on the world, for all seeking to change opinions and for all wanting to transform the nature of a discussion, Twitter and blogs are powerful tools. But it is worthwhile taking the time to figure out how to do it well. A good initial strategy is simply to 'retweet' other people; and to promote admirable viewpoints – or events that seem important and interesting. This starting-point helps to build a following, and reveals those who retweet in response.

There is also a mass of expertise out there, willing to help. Whether it is a problematic bit of palaeography, or a question of the best background reading for a new subject, tagging a question with #twitterstorian or just asking a general audience will frequently generate a helpful response. If the question is personal, or the details become too arcane, then it's fine to ask people to communicate by 'direct message'.

Eventually, staying active on a platform for a sufficient period of time allows the building of a good group of friendly followers. Researchers can present their own work and provide information about dates/venues for their presentations. It is important not to do this too much – as there is nothing worse than the appearance of online braggadocio. However, letting others know about research presentations is a community service and helps to ensure that there is a live audience, as well as one online.

8.5 Coping with trolls

Those who participate online long enough will come across trolls, who love to foment discord.[4] Every individual who contributes will eventually get the tone or content wrong and come under attack online. Indeed, the more followers a researcher attracts, and the more posts that are made, the more difficult it is to avoid occasionally getting into trouble. In the event of making an error, the best thing is to apologize immediately and move on. Twitter has a short memory, even if Tweets have a long shelf-life.

Yet sometimes further action is required. In the first instance, anyone being trolled should immediately 'unfollow' the trollers; or, more decisively, 'block' them. Historians want to have open conversations which include a variety of voices, but a degree of self-protection is necessary. If some posts are particularly triggering of discord, then there is no need to give them screen space. And if they move towards hate speech, they should be reported. There are a huge variety of internet trolls, from alt-right extremists, to purer-than-the-driven-snow leftists, always happy to point out everyone else's moral flaws. The best moment to stop listening is when the conversation is generating anxiety or depression.

Social media is meant to facilitate conversation that is not only fruitful but fun; and, when the fun stops, it is time to leave. (See also section 13.5.) Creativity needs silence and space as well as buzz and shared stimulus.

8.6 Summary: writing snout to tail

As already stressed (see section 7.3), historians write constantly. If all social media does is distract from the task in hand – if too much time is spent looking at pictures of kittens or of fancy meals – then social media emphatically won't help the completion of a large piece of research. But it is possible to build social media into the writing process, and, by using it creatively, to generate excitement about the project. At an extreme, social media can be used to test ideas and to ask for response: *'Is it crazy to think that …?' 'Is there evidence for …?' 'Have I missed sources on …?'*

Still more useful are blogs. Either personal blogs, or collective blogs which invite contributions, allow researchers to try out longer pieces of writing, and to measure responses. The 'Many-Headed Monster', for example, is a collective blog about early modern British social history, which regularly solicits contributions and has become one of the main venues where the field

---

[4] P. Fichman and M. Sanfilippo, *Online Trolling and Its Perpetrators: Under the Cyberbridge* (Lanham, Md., 2016); A. Salter and B. Blodgett, *Toxic Geek Masculinity in Media: Sexism, Trolling and Identity Policing* (Basingstoke, 2017); T. Flynn, *Rage-In: the Trolls and Tribulations of Modern Life* (Cork, 2018).

is discussed.[5] But even posting the text of a conference paper to a personal blog will help generate an audience and build a following – particularly if it's matched with a link on Twitter. Posting online also has the advantage of ensuring that authors write with an awareness that a wider audience might be reading.

When researchers write only for their supervisors and a few close friends, it is easy to assume they will forgive complex prose, because they recognize that the ideas being expressed are complex. But when all the world might be reading, there is a stronger motive to get the style right: intelligent but not abstruse. Writing regularly also inculcates the habit, and saves authors from the preciousness that many initially feel about exposing their writing to others. Writing well is frequently just a matter of practice.

Many younger scholars worry that publishing their ideas too soon will harm their reputation, or allow someone else to steal their ideas and hard-won research insights. Yet publishing in any form, including in blog posts, provides a demonstrable authorship that no-one can steal. It is entirely legitimate to re-use a blog post as part of a doctorate or a peer-reviewed publication (with the addition of an appropriate level of footnoting and academic apparatus).

Blogging also has the advantage of gradually building a familiar audience. By the time it comes to give a paper in a seminar or conference – or later, after the award of a degree, to publish the book of the thesis – the audience will be primed and eager to read the outcome. The historians' role is changing, and the ways in which they reach an audience have evolved to include social media. Being self-aware online enables researchers to participate in a shared intellectual community, and simultaneously to ensure that their own contributions are valued and recognized.

[5] See <https://manyheadedmonster.com/> [accessed 24 January 2022].

9. Unblocking writer's block or, better still, non-blocking in the first place

Barriers to effective research and writing can be overcome with the aid of friends, mentors and known techniques of recovery.

9.1 Avoiding writer's block

During every big project, researchers may find themselves at some stage confronted by a blank screen and a blank mind. For some, this experience can lead to real emotional anxiety and a kind of intellectual paralysis. In response, the best advice is not to work in complete isolation.

Ultimately, much researching and almost all writing are processes which are undertaken by individuals on their own – the growing number of collective projects notwithstanding. But if these tasks are done with positive support from a community of fellow researchers – and pursued within regular and well-monitored writing deadlines – the pressures are lightened.[1] That's why students should remain in close touch not only with their supervisors but also with their peer group. And a good means of remaining in contact with others is to participate actively in a regular academic seminar (see chapter 14).

At the same time, common sense advises that due care should always be taken to remain physically and mentally well. Active, agile minds need a bit of exercise, as do the bodies they inhabit. So all the good advice, dispensed to the world in general, is equally relevant for researchers. It's sensible to sleep deeply, eat sensibly and refrain from smoking, taking drugs and drinking alcohol to excess. And it's worth recollecting that the myths about booze and creativity are indeed myths.[2]

Stirring physical activities form a positive and integral counterpart to intellectual efforts.[3] Exercising regularly is particularly valuable. It constantly recharges both mental and physical batteries. Many authors report upon the benefits they get from repetitive, rhythmic activities which do not require much conscious self-direction, such as swimming, riding, running, going to the gym and walking. And for those who cannot undertake strenuous exercise, or find time to go for a walk, then gentle stretching has significant health benefits.[4] Doing as much as possible is the key, allowing for different individual circumstances. Such repetitive and 'mindless' bodily exercises allow the conscious mind to rest and set the subconscious free to mull over problems, in a non-linear way. Often after a period of such lateral thinking, an answer to a contentious issue will present itself unbidden. And, even if not, the complexities have been explored and can be explained to others.

All repetitive exercises have a positive effect if sustained for at least half an hour – daily. But, to repeat, fitness is recommended as a help, but certainly not as a pre-requisite, for historians. The admirable Margaret Spufford, who coped stoically with ill-health all her life, also managed to write path-breaking historical studies. She provides an outstanding example of the power of the mind (with loving support from her family) to triumph over adversity.[5] In

---

[1] S. Johnson, *The Writer's Toolkit: Banish the Curse of Writer's Block* (Pershore, 2005).

[2] D. W. Goodwin, *Alcohol and the Writer* (Kansas City, Mo., 1988).

[3] K. O'Neill (ed.), *Bringing Together Physical and Mental Health: a New Frontier for Integrated Care* (London, 2016); L. C. W. Lam et al. (ed.), *Physical Exercise Interventions for Mental Health* (Cambridge, 2019).

[4] S. Martin, *Stretching: the Stress-Free Way to Stay Supple, Keep Fit and Exercise Safely* (London, 2005).

[5] M. Spufford, *Contrasting Communities: English Villagers in the Sixteenth and Seventeenth Centuries* (Cambridge, 1974); M. Spufford, *Small Books and Pleasant Histories: Popular*

sum, therefore, researchers are encouraged to seek the mental benefits of suitable exercise, within the bounds of their personal circumstances.

9.2 Myths and realities of writer's block

From time to time, however, some writers feel creatively locked. It's not a good state of mind, although it should be stressed that it's not an inevitable stage of research. It used to be more common, before methods of supervision were tightened. The authors of this *Guide* view writing as a craft skill, which can be learned and polished without too much anxiety.

Yet momentum can at times be lost. And, left untreated, writer's block can lead to frustration, guilt, irritable self-chastisement and various degrees of despair.[6] Blocked writers particularly wince when bystanders ask cheerfully: 'How's the writing going?' Their probing goodwill has the effect of pressing upon a tender bruise. And, while casual enquiries can be deflected, things get worse if close friends and family continue to enquire reproachfully: 'Why isn't it done yet?'

Some blocked writers cannot even bear to admit the existence of a difficulty, while others tell everyone. Neither response is helpful. Creative agony can be very debilitating. It can make people physically ill or socially depressive. There are well-known fictional exemplars. In George Eliot's *Middlemarch* (1871/2), the unwritten masterpiece of the learned Dr Casaubon becomes a groaning incubus which blights his marriage and all his relationships. His quest for a 'perfect' and fully comprehensive study has filled him with a sapping dread of failure.[7] There are also well-documented real-life cases. F. Scott Fitzgerald's wry account of his inability to write in *The Crack-Up* (1936) is as painful to read as he meant it to be.[8]

Fiction and Its Readership in Seventeenth-Century England (London, 1981); M. Spufford, *The Great Reclothing of Rural England: Petty Chapmen and Their Wares in the Seventeenth Century* (London, 1984); M. Spufford, *Figures in the Landscape: Rural Society in England, 1500–7000* (Aldershot, 2000); and, published after her death, M. Spufford and S. Mee, *The Clothing of the Common Sort, 1570–1700* (New York, 2017).

[6] A. W. Flaherty, *The Midnight Disease: the Drive to Write, Writer's Block, and the Creative Brain* (Boston, Mass., 2004); J. Flanders, *Writer's Block* (London, 2014).

[7] G. Eliot, *Middlemarch* (London, 1871/2): there has been much speculation about the real-life original, if any, of Dr Casaubon. Most commentators view him as a dry old stick, who is a blight upon his ardent young wife. But for a bravura counter-attack, see N. Ascherson, 'The truth about Casaubon: a great intellect destroyed by a silly woman', *The Independent*, 20 Feb. 1994: <https://web.archive.org/web/20201218134927/http://www.independent.co.uk:80/voices/the-truth-about-casaubon-a-great-intellect-destroyed-by-a-silly-woman-1395385.html> [accessed 9 Feb. 2022].

[8] F. S. Fitzgerald, *The Stories of F. Scott Fitzgerald, Vol. II: the Crack-Up with Other Pieces and Stories* (Harmondsworth, 1965), pp. 39–56.

And later, the blocked travel-writer Patrick Leigh Fermor, who wrote two splendid books of a planned trilogy, fretted for years over his failure to complete the third.[9]

These cases carry an implicit warning that the problem, left unchecked, grows worse, not better. But it is important not to become too tragic about writer's block. A programme of regular writing, for regular inspection by a helpful supervisor, should prevent the problem from developing (as explained in chapter 3).

Ultimately, people tend to write what they want to write. One eminent Victorian sage who is often quoted in this context was Lord Acton, the Regius Professor of History at Cambridge. His 'History of Liberty' became famed for never being written, despite a lifetime of planning. Instead, it was Acton's essays and epigrams, many of them published posthumously, which have survived. In particular, one key maxim is widely quoted to this day. Acton's warning that '[All] power tends to corrupt; and absolute power corrupts absolutely'[10] has reached far more people than the rest of his work. Thus, brief but apt contributions have a role. Acton's distinguished academic life was by no means a disaster. Authors have varied work preferences, and produce very varied outputs – a key point always worth bearing in mind.

9.3 Moments for reassessment

In general, then, researchers should watch their step, in order not to fall into what John Bunyan identified as 'the Slough of Despond' that lurks to trap the unwary on life's journey.[11] However, should a period of blockage develop, then it's best to take stock instantly. Letting the problem fester only makes it worse. An immediate question is whether the blockage, in reality, means that the researcher really wants to do something else entirely. In practice, it's not always possible to change. Nonetheless, a proportion of blocked people who do switch projects mid-stream find that the move can unleash hitherto thwarted energy. A blockage in one direction may thus dissolve once the route has been changed.

Alternatively, another step is to reassess the nature of the writing task, around which the blockage has formed. Can the exposition be done in a

---

[9] Published posthumously from his notebooks: see P. L. Fermor, *The Broken Road: From the Iron Gates to Mount Athos*, ed. C. Thubron and A. Cooper (London, 2013), following *A Time of Gifts* (London, 1977) and *Between the Woods and the Water* (London, 1986).

[10] Letter from Lord Acton (April 1887) in *Historical Essays and Studies by John Emerich Edward Dalberg-Acton*, ed. J. N. Figgis and R. V. Laurence (London, 1907), p. 504. For context, see also O. Chadwick, *Acton and History* (Cambridge, 1998).

[11] An evocative concept from the classic J. Bunyan, *Pilgrim's Progress* (London, 1678).

different way? Taking time out to reconsider and replan can promote renewal. And, if the blockage relates to one big section of the argument, it's worth checking whether the task can be sub-divided into many discrete and smaller components. Breaking down an apparently forbidding 'mountain' of work into manageable chunks can immediately reduce the problem.

One variant of that stratagem invites the researcher to assemble the underlying evidence and quotations in a sequence that makes an argument. It's the equivalent of creating a framework which can then be filled in gradually, rather than all in a rush. Step-by-step writing is a good way of demystifying the production process.

Practically, too, it can be helpful to have a break from past locations which are associated with anguish and failure. A new venue for writing or a significant new arrangement of an established work area can be used as a marker of recovery and renewal. Whatever works.

Meanwhile, it must not be overlooked that writing problems may be symptomatic of deeper psychological problems. If expert help is seriously required, then there is only benefit from seeking professional assistance without delay. Supervisors and friends can help up to a point; but they are not trained therapists. All higher education institutions these days have dedicated support services with mental health professionals. The old taboos about admitting the need for mental health counselling are dissolving. If necessary, therefore, researchers should not hesitate to get professional help. The depth of writers' despair over their inability to write is often a tribute to their basic motivation – and their annoyance that things have stalled. As a result, getting practical help can turn these moments of reassessment into fruitful turning-points.

9.4 Expressive writing therapy

A writing therapy that works for many people, but not for all, can also be tried at this point. It invites researchers to pen, rapidly and spontaneously, a stream-of-consciousness memorandum, which is not to be viewed by any other person. In other words, it's a form of auto-communing on paper. Often blocked writing turns out to be caused by genuinely tricky intellectual issues. Much historical analysis requires juggling multiple themes and many forms of evidence all at once. Managing to pull everything together can prove overwhelming. Thoughts go round and round, without cohering. And a small stumbling block can become slowly magnified into something much larger.

Writing a stream-of-consciousness (known for short as a 'streamo') should be done in an unstructured style. Grammatical faults and spelling mistakes can remain uncorrected. No-one else need ever see this screed. It inverts the problem of not writing by writing a large amount very quickly. And it's devised as a way of interrogating one's own thoughts: *What is the basic problem that is causing this block? Is it this? Is it that?* It may well take a long time to work through all the issues. But that's all to the good. Simply sitting and musing on problems is not sufficiently disciplined. The mind flits too readily from topic to topic. Torrential writing is intended to dredge up thoughts and then to examine them. In this way, blocked authors are not asked to write measured and publishable prose – which is proving too hard a task. Instead, they are encouraged to unleash words and thoughts chaotically.

Sometimes people prefer to write their streamos in the form of detailed jottings. Others find that listed points, which are very helpful when summarizing tasks to be done, are not as productive as consecutive prose for assessing intellectual difficulties. However, any form of rapid writing will do. Having undertaken such intellectual self-pummelling, researchers will discover whether the problem at the heart of the difficulty was mundane or complex. Either way, it's a relief to know. Researchers sigh to themselves: *'So that's it'*. Then the mind signals to itself that it is time to quit the blockage. Authors can resume their main writing task, armed with fresh thoughts and new answers. They can point explicitly to the relevant intellectual problem – and explain how it can be resolved. It takes a bit of time to get a critical distance on one's own problems. Yet there's poetic justice in this method.

After a period of intensive self-examination, unblocked by rapid free writing, the difficulty can then become simply an issue for analysis within the overall discussion. Thus a helpful general rule states that: *if there is a problem, then researchers do well not to brood on it – but instead to write it down.*

To repeat, stream-of-consciousness memoranda can play a useful role in intellectual unblocking. These techniques are advocated in therapy as a powerful means of mental release and finding of inner calm.[12] Such formats also have a known place in fiction, whereby people's inner worlds are illuminated by a stream-of-consciousness.[13] Of course, it cannot be claimed that one method of unblocking will help everyone equally. But

---

[12] H. M. Vyner, *The Healthy Mind: Mindfulness, the True Self and the Stream of Consciousness* (London, 2018); H. S. Schroder, T. P. Moran and J. S. Moser, 'The effect of expressive writing on the error-related negativity among individuals with chronic worry', *Psychophysiology*, lv (2018): <https://www.researchgate.net/publication/319558646> [accessed 3 May 2021].

[13] See, eg, R. Humphrey, *Stream of Consciousness in the Modern Novel* (Berkeley, Calif., 1954; Cambridge, 1958).

getting a realistic insight into one's own inner world can help to demystify the romantic 'agony' and to turn recovery into a practical exercise.

9.5 Summary: historical research and lifestyle choices

Becoming a historian is ultimately a lifestyle choice as well as everything else. Researching, writing, debating, exercising and keeping as fit as possible (given personal circumstances) ideally go together as a combined package.

Therefore, writing blockages, if encountered, should be tackled as soon as possible. Energy then floods in once the obstacles have been cleared. It goes without saying that it is best not to have such problems. Yet, if things do go wrong, there are known ways of coping.

Moreover, those who have recovered have learned a key lesson in surmounting difficulties. Lord Acton once remarked pointedly, perhaps with some personal reference while not writing his long-expected big book: 'Praise is the shipwreck of historians'.[14] Conversely, those who have nearly capsized through agony, doubt and self-blame have suffered the reverse of praise. Too much criticism and auto-criticism can also be shipwrecking. Yet overcoming intellectual doubt and adversity is supremely educational. It can not only rekindle but positively enhance the research flame.

---

[14] J. E. E. Dalberg-Acton, 'The study of history: inaugural lecture' (London, 1895), in Dalberg-Acton, *Lectures on Modern History* (London, 1930 edn), p. 28.

10. Using technology creatively: digital history

SIGNPOST: Relevant to all researchers

The bold and beautiful tiger, bursting through the barriers, is a symbol for the computing power of digital history updating traditional research processes.

10.1 Non-stop learning

Whether the research project focuses upon the history of poetry or economics – whether it is about gender, discourse, diplomacy or cash flows – the way historians analyse their sources has changed substantially in the last thirty years.[1] As a large (though selective) proportion of inherited print and manuscripts have been digitized, all historians have become 'digital'.

---

[1] For overviews, see Levenberg, Neilson and Rheams (ed.), *Research Methods for the Digital Humanities*; Milligan, *History in the Age of Abundance*; Salmi, *What Is Digital History?*; and Crymble, *Technology and the Historian*.

They access many of their sources as digital files and write history while sitting in front of a screen.

Furthermore, 'born digital' sources are increasingly important, and images that were traditionally inaccessible in museum collections are now much more available – and available for analysis – in digital form. For most historians, 'the object of study' (whatever its nature) is often now a collection of digital files. As a result, and however well or awkwardly they manage, all who study the past are 'digital historians' now.

A whole new series of tools and approaches to analysing this new data has emerged. Most are available online and all involve some form of computational analysis. Many methodologies have been borrowed from other disciplines. Corpus Linguistics (the statistical analysis of large bodies of text) allows historians to review inherited texts in new ways, while geography brings its knowledge of space and mapping, via sophisticated Geographical Information Systems (GIS). Computer science also adds techniques like 'topic modelling', network analysis and the statistical analysis of graphics files. And the broader world of 'big data' has lent tools for the organization and cross-analysis of all forms of historical evidence.

For historians, the big challenge is to know what tools to use – and, equally, how much effort to expend in learning how to use them. Most researchers into the past don't want to specialize as computer programmers and/or as geographers.

Hence it's crucial to know where to find good advice and, simultaneously, to know when to get back to the archive or the original source deposit. In other words, historians need to have enough information to make the right choices. Digital history must be done well, and neither misused or confused.

10.2 The Programming Historian

The single best starting-point for anyone seeking to use digital methodologies when working with historical materials is *The Programming Historian* (*PH*).[2] This admirable resource is now published in three languages (English, French and Spanish). It presents dozens of tutorials, written by historians, and specifically designed to support fellow researchers. Users can thus identify the most helpful tools, and develop the basic skills to apply them credibly.

Started in 2008 by William Turkel and Alan MacEachern, the *PH* has grown into a major international initiative. It is staffed by volunteers; and,

---

[2] <https://programminghistorian.org> [accessed 30 April 2021].

year by year, it augments and revises its set of tutorials. Currently, there are 150 published tutorials, ranging from an 'Intro to Google Maps and Google Earth' and an 'Introduction to Jupyter Notebooks' to more advanced topics like 'Manipulating Strings in Python'. Each tutorial is built around historical data and should take no more than an hour or so to process.

Most historians will not need to work through more than a handful of tutorials to undertake all the data-processing jobs required by a substantial research project. But it is worth getting to know what is available; and it's advisable to return to the *PH* when confronted by a new task or data challenge.

Some will want to become expert in one specific technique or approach. The most important thing, however, is a willingness to investigate. Researchers should be open to learning what they need, as and when they need it. Sampling a few tutorials is a fine way to explore the options and to check whether any specific approach will be useful.

Needless to say, the perennial advice given to researchers also applies in this case. Always check the time/benefit analysis. It's vital not to overlook crucial research tools – just as it's disastrous to embark on some great but labour-intensive approach, which will take longer than the time available for the project. Here, advice from fellow researchers and supervisors can be invaluable.

10.3 Text as data

Much historical research involves reading 'text', whether this takes the form of published books and newspapers, manuscript archives or a million Tweets. And in all cases where the texts have been digitized (or emerged 'born digital'), they have become a form of 'data'. That is, they constitute strings of code, which can be analysed at scale.

This new characteristic of inherited (historic) texts has provided one of the great 'affordances' of modern scholarship, creating a large number of new opportunities. Being able to count how historical language changes over time is remarkably revealing. To take a single example, an analysis, showing how different vocabularies are used to describe men and women's work across different sources, offers a powerful reflection upon the workings of patriarchy.[3] Or a study tracing the spread of new technologies (through the occurrence of the new words used to describe it) would serve as a way of illustrating broader trends in changing socio-cultural attitudes.

---

[3] See J. Holmes, *Gendered Talk at Work: Constructing Gender Identity through Workplace Discourse* (Oxford, 2006); and context in J. M. Bennett, *History Matters: Patriarchy and the Challenge of Feminism* (Philadelphia, Pa., 2006).

At its simplest, moreover, counting the frequency of words in a single article will help to elucidate its core message. A quick and straightforward way of testing changing language over time is provided by the Google Ngram Viewer.[4] This tool allows researchers to chart the frequency of any word they choose against a large corpus of published text. Entering a simple search string, such as 'iron, steel', and charting its usage against English publications since 1700 would provide a rapid measure of evolving industrialization. Meanwhile, for those wishing to make a quick check for leads in the archive of Western texts, the Ngram Viewer also works well. Yet most historians work on a more specific collection of materials. Hence researchers need to create a collection or 'corpus' of texts for their own purposes.

Before starting, it's essential to ensure that the chosen 'text' is useable and consistent. Many digital resources online provide only an image of a page rather than transcribed texts, making it hard to generate a reliable corpus for advanced study. If the pages are printed, it is normally possible to use an Optical Character Recognition (OCR) tool, of the sort that is available in common PDF readers such as Adobe Acrobat.[5]

However, manuscripts – if not already transcribed by someone else – will require a different approach. Even web resources that provide a digital text are frequently of poor quality. A source such as the *Burney Collection of Seventeenth- and Eighteenth-Century Newspapers*, for instance, which provides both images of the original page and OCRd text for searching and analysis, is marred by an almost unacceptable error rate. In the underlying text used for searches, less than half of all semantically significant words are accurately transcribed.[6] Errors generally arise from lack of visual clarity in the original eighteenth-century printed pages, which can often be faded and tattered. These kinds of transcribed sources – including Google Books – are still useable, since the scale of the collections makes topics findable, even given the errors. Nonetheless, researchers need to understand their intrinsic level of errors.

Once having established the extent of precision required, researchers then need either manually to gather the material in which they are interested; or, alternatively, to 'scrape' a site automatically to collect relevant elements.

    4 <https://books.google.com/ngrams> [accessed 30 April 2021].
    5 For Adobe Acrobat, see: <https://www.adobe.com/uk/> [accessed 25 March 2022].
    6 S. Tanner, T. Muñoz and P. H. Ros, 'Measuring mass text digitization quality and usefulness: lessons learned from assessing the OCR accuracy of the British Library's nineteenth-century online newspaper archive', *D-Lib Magazine* (2009): <https://doi .org/10.1045/july2009-munoz> [accessed 30 April 2021].

The Programming Historian has several tutorials that can help. And, when working with published books, some organizations such as the Hathi Trust Digital Library[7] can also provide accurately transcribed texts.

Then researchers need an appropriate set of tools that will allow them to interrogate the corpus. An easy way to begin is using an online environment such as Voyant Tools.[8] Created by Stéfan Sinclair and Geoffrey Rockwell, Voyant allows researchers simply to copy and paste any text into an online box, or to upload a file or set of files from their own computers, or to enter a URL for a public website. Voyant will then provide a set of word frequency tables and visualizations that will help to reveal underlying patterns.

10.4 Quantitative data as data

More regular data, whether entries in an account book, Parliamentary returns or any form of consistent record for that matter, will also benefit from analysis using either a database or spreadsheet. As with text, the most important first step is to know the data. Some projects are based around a deep engagement with a single source; and, in such cases, it is very helpful to survey the full range of material available from beginning to end, before deciding precisely what technology to use. Even apparently consistent series of records tend to change subtly decade by decade. Other projects build upon a variety of sources about a single topic or individual, and often involve working with a range of different discrete datasets. Again, researchers should engage closely with the material and then consider the basic options. The first decision is how to get the data from the historical records into a useable form; and the second is what 'package', or set of tools, to use in their analysis and visualization.

Two basic approaches to data organization take the form of databases and spreadsheets. The first has traditionally been used for recording textual and mixed textual/numeric data, while the latter evolved from accounting and is associated with recording detailed numerical data. In fact, however, both databases and spreadsheets do almost precisely the same job, and do it in very much the same way. Underlying both is a series of 'cells' or 'fields' that collectively and in their raw form appear as a simple table, with each row representing a separate item, and each column a category of information. Data from either can then be exported into a straightforward CSV format that can in turn be used in any data-processing package.

[7] <https://www.hathitrust.org> [accessed 30 April 2021].
[8] <https://voyant-tools.org> [accessed 29 April 2021].

Databases have the great advantage that they facilitate data entry – researchers can easily design a bespoke data entry 'form' for this purpose. Yet databases do not lend themselves readily to statistical analysis. In contrast, spreadsheets such as Excel are slow to populate with accurate data, but tend to include more tools for manipulating and analysing the data. Whichever is chosen, it remains essential to be as true to the original sources as possible.

It is worthwhile starting with a simple exercise, such as creating a table in Word and seeing how easy (or otherwise) it is to populate with information. The process of entering just a few pages of historical materials will reveal key problems with labels and categories, and allow further consideration before completion. It is crucial to ensure that basic classifications can be trusted and shared with other researchers. Idiosyncratic inventions may seem fun at the time, but are valueless if rejected as meaningless by other researchers.

There will always be 'edge cases' – instances that can fall into more than one category, or which are simply ambiguous – but a good understanding of the material will help keep those to a minimum. It is also vital to respect the sources, and to include as much data as possible. When starting out, it is easy to assume that the initial questions should limit what is transcribed. But including as much data as possible – even when it initially seems tangential – will make the data more robust and also more capable of being re-used. Research questions change in the course of study, and data that seemed irrelevant at the start could well be crucial in the end.

Having decided how much data to record and in what format, the next step is to determine how best to enter it. This process can be tedious beyond measure. Here databases have an initial advantage, in that it is relatively easy to create a bespoke 'data entry form'. And entering data into a well-designed template – tabbing from field to field – is infinitely less irritating than trying to navigate a spreadsheet. At the same time, however, spreadsheets will also allow researchers to create a data entry 'template', and it is worth doing so.

For some purposes, regular data is already available. The UK Data Archive[9] and services such as Zenodo[10] hold thousands of datasets that can be downloaded and re-used for free. And while other people's data is never quite right, and will need to be adapted and cleaned in services such as Open Refine,[11] it is always worth checking what is available before sitting down to build a new dataset. Incidentally, gaining access to data held by commercial companies such as FindMyPast.co.uk and Ancestry.co.uk is much more difficult, but always worth a try.

9 <https://www.data-archive.ac.uk> [accessed 30 April 2021].
10 <https://zenodo.org> [accessed 30 April 2021].
11 <https://openrefine.org> [accessed 30 April 2021].

Whether, in the end, the decision is to re-use already established datasets, or to create a simple spreadsheet, or to populate a complex relational database, the next step is to see what the data says; and for such analysis, different tools are needed. Traditionally, very large social science datasets were analysed using SPSS (originally devised as a 'Statistical Package for the Social Sciences', and now renamed as 'Statistical Product and Service Solutions').[12] But for most historians, who do not work with huge social science datasets, using SPSS results in overkill. Instead, the in-built tools within spreadsheets, such as Excel, usually prove more than adequate.

Moreover, because both spreadsheets and databases export to common formats such as CSV, data first created in them can be re-used in more flexible visualization environments. Examples include Gephi, which is an open source for visualization of graphs and networks,[13] and the appealingly named 'Many Eyes'.[14] Historians working on networks, in particular, have found in Gephi an all-important set of tools. But requirements are always changing, so it's helpful to survey the options regularly.

10.5 Space and place

Geographical information has in particular attracted its own sophisticated set of tools and research environments. From the early 1960s, geographers began to develop a series of conventions and tools for working with computers that eventually evolved into a set of distinct approaches and a suite of commercial software. At its most sophisticated, this software has become intimidatingly complex and expensive to access. Nevertheless, it does allow researchers to manipulate and analyse specific locations and polygons, defining areas on the globe, and to layer sets of data one over the other, in order to reveal patterns.

Across all the natural sciences, GIS (Geographic Information Systems) in particular has become an indispensable tool. And if individual researchers do not have access to the software via an educational institution, then there is also a free version, QGIS.[15] The welcome ubiquity of this tool is a sign of the enhanced importance given to space and place in all forms of analysis.[16]

---

[12] G. Argyrous, *Statistics for Research: With a Guide to SPSS* (London, 2005).

[13] <https://gephi.org> [accessed 30 April 2021].

[14] <https://boostlabs.com/blog/ibms-many-eyes-online-data-visualization-tool> [accessed 30 April 2021].

[15] <https://qgis.org/en/site> [accessed 30 April 2021].

[16] Some historians have always been concerned with space and place; but for the recent enhanced interest, see T. Zeller, 'The spatial turn in history', *Bulletin of the German Historical Institute*, xxxv (2004), 123–4; B. Worf and S. Arias (ed.), *The Spatial Turn: Interdisciplinary Perspectives* (London, 2009); R. T. Tally, *Spatiality* (London, 2013).

Historians who are taking their first steps down this road can meanwhile find simpler solutions. Google Earth[17] makes possible the mapping of most types of simple data, while sites such as BatchGeo[18] allow lists of addresses to be turned into specific geo-references, which can then be mapped. Once again, too, *The Programming Historian* has several tutorials that can help.

Undoubtedly, one of the great advantages of working with geographical data is that there is simply a huge amount of it out there; and much of it is free to use. Geographical data can also be exported to a CSV format and analysed in combination with other varieties of information.

Historical maps are particularly vital sources of geographical data. These have long been used and exploited by historians, but are now increasingly available online, and in a 'warped' format – that is, stretched to reflect existing geography. A site such as Old Maps Online[19] gives access to over 400,000 historical maps, held in over forty-five libraries and archives. Most can also be viewed as an overlay on a modern map, and many can be imported into Google Earth for further manipulation. As a result, sensitivity to place can now be readily incorporated into historical analysis, not as an optional extra but as integral.

10.6 The delights and dangers of data

Digital history provides massively useful tools for historians. But there's no need to become a computer scientist in order to wield these tools. And there's no need to fear them either. Adding a map, citing a word frequency or including a graph simply makes a good historical study all the more compelling.

Indeed, mastering at least some digital tools is a liberating experience. New applications become apparent. New connections between old sources and new techniques are made possible. A list suddenly suggests itself as a map; a set of texts becomes a corpus; and a collection of letters, a virtual network.

Remember, however, that history-writing is a craft. Digital techniques help towards making useful steps on the journey. They are not ends in themselves. Historians strive to inform and influence their readers, not to stun or dazzle them with methodology.

Easily processed data, resulting in 'shock and awe' graphics, is seductive. It is easy to be impressed by the sheer scale of some datasets, and to assume that any patterns revealed must be significant. But researchers must always

[17] <https://earth.google.com/web> [accessed 30 April 2021].
[18] <https://batchgeo.com> [accessed 30 April 2021].
[19] <https://www.oldmapsonline.org> [accessed 30 April 2021].

remain wary. There are biases within all sources which have been digitized. And the historian's first task remains to identify and to make interpretative allowances for such in-built biases. Otherwise, the smart new techno-data is simply magnifying (and possibly obscuring) old limitations within the data.

To take a single example, an exciting project like *Mapping the Republic of Letters*[20] is based on 20,000 letters, written by major figures of the European Enlightenment. However, the choice of letters for digitization was determined by what was already available in print (largely early to mid twentieth-century publications). Hence, editorial decisions, made in the 1950s and earlier, have been given new currency; and the racial and gender biases (whether implicit or sometimes explicit) of a long-superseded scholarship have been reinforced. What appears at first sight to be new research at the cutting edge of technology frequently turns out to reproduce older, Euro-centric histories. Historians should therefore cultivate the skill of interrogating silences in the archives – and looking hard for alternative forms of evidence.[21]

In addition, search algorithms often incorporate unstated biases, such as outdated assumptions about 'race'. One popular tool for identifying patterns in large corpora is called 'Mallet'. It identifies 'topics' using a complex algorithm that measures word frequency and co-location. The problem for all researchers is that Mallet – and 'topic modelling' in general[22] – works as a black-box system, which obscures its working criteria. Their results can appear compelling, producing lists of seemingly related words, which may then be identified as 'topics' by researchers. But few understand the algorithms involved, so that most accept the results without really understanding how they were generated.

Ultimately, the best and only response for researchers is to know their sources; and to know what questions they are posing – and why. Those crucial requirements are more vital than ever when the data is being fed en masse into machines, whose workings are frequently opaque. In the current media-dominated world, the bombardment of data and images can become vertiginous. Indeed, cultural critics like Jean Baudrillard worry that not just historians but all citizens will become confused into a state

---

[20] <http://republicofletters.stanford.edu> [accessed 30 April 2021].

[21] On missing or concealed evidence, see Johnson, Fowler and Thomas, *The Silence of the Archive*.

[22] See M. R. Brett, 'Topic modelling: a basic introduction', *Journal of Digital Humanities*, ii (2012): <http://journalofdigitalhumanities.org/2-1/topic-modeling-a-basic-introduction-by-megan-r-brett> [accessed 30 April 2021]; and Leetaru, *Data Mining Methods*.

of 'hyper-reality', indistinguishable from the real thing.[23] Hence everyone should cultivate a good countervailing sense of scepticism. And all should avoid the trap of uncritical techno-worship. That danger was noted by Lewis Mumford in 1962[24] when he warned that:

> minds unduly fascinated by computers carefully confine themselves to asking only the kind of question that computers can answer and are completely negligent of the human contents or the human results.

In other words, historical researchers, and not their research tools, are the ones who produce research – and the ones who bear responsibility for the outcomes.

[23] R. G. Smith and D. B. Clarke (ed.), *Jean Baudrillard: From Hyper-Reality to Disappearance – Uncollected Interviews* (Edinburgh, 2015).
[24] L. Mumford, 'The sky line "Mother Jacobs home remedies"', *The New Yorker*, 1 Dec. 1962, 148.

11. Assessing some key research approaches

SIGNPOST: Relevant to all researchers

Untangling research knots.

11.1 'Soft' or qualitative interpretations

'Soft' or qualitative interpretations, especially in social and cultural history, focus chiefly upon meanings and significance, rather than quantity and scale. As already noted, they do not necessarily supply 'easy' or 'self-indulgent' answers. But 'soft' techniques do deal in interpretations and subjective views, rather than in 'hard' statistics and impersonal analysis.

In caricature, there is a sharp polar dichotomy in these ways of knowing. 'Soft' emotion sobs or cheers, while 'hard' reason analyses. In practice, however, deep thought combines both subjective and objective elements.[1]

There is no reason, therefore, to shy away from 'soft' qualitative techniques, if undertaken with rational care. This chapter analyses the strengths and

[1] A. R. Damascio, *Descartes' Error: Emotions, Reason and the Human Brain* (London, 2006).

weaknesses of key approaches, showing how to get the best out of exercises in historical empathy; oral history; prosopography or group biographies; reading the silences; and 'thick' cultural description. A final section considers the study of history's What Ifs, known as counterfactual analysis, which can be undertaken by using both 'hard' statistics and 'soft' intuitions. All these approaches can be used singly or in combination, as appropriate.

11.2 Empathy

'Empathy' tends to polarize opinion, partly because it can easily be misunderstood. John Major, as British prime minister, once unwisely urged, with reference to criminals, that society should 'condemn more, understand less'.[2] But condemnation and comprehension are never polar opposites. A better understanding of despicable or dangerous behaviour provides better options for averting/changing/treating/punishing such manifestations. Empathy, after all, differs from sympathy. That warm, positive emotion entails sharing and resonating positively with a given set of views or actions. Empathy, by contrast, calls for a cool intellectual/emotional understanding, without either condoning or sympathizing.[3] It calls for effort to 'get inside the mind' of others, however strange or alien their views and lifestyles may be.

A common application of empathy techniques is used to study the opposing sides in wars or civil conflicts. It is important to understand history's 'baddies' and 'losers' as well as its 'goodies' and 'winners'. (Indeed, those categories are often jumbled.) One problem for empathy exercises relating to societies before the advent of mass literacy lies in the limited evidence relating to personal motivations. Equally, historians need to acknowledge that the great bulk of written evidence, even when purporting to describe private feelings, is first and foremost designed to be read by others. Researchers seeking to reconstruct past feelings have therefore to recognize the potential gulf between what people say or write and what they experience inwardly.

Nonetheless, historians use their ingenuity to find whatever sources they can. And they also use proxy measures, by looking at people's actions and (with caution) their inactions. A fine example is provided by Nicholas

---

[2] John Major (PM 1990–7), as reported in *The Independent*, 21 Feb. 1993: <https://www.independent.co.uk/news/major-on-crime-condemn-more-understand-less-1474470.html> [accessed 30 April 2021].

[3] T. Retz, *Empathy and History: Historical Understanding in Re-enactment, Hermeneutics and Education* (New York, 2018); P. Towle, *History, Empathy and Conflict: Heroes, Victims and Victimisers* (Basingstoke, 2018).

Stargardt in his study of ordinary Germans in the Second World War.[4] The author's intense recoil from Nazism is the bedrock upon which a judicious superstructure of applied empathy is based, using diaries, letters, recollections and other sources.

At one time, the historian R. G. Collingwood even defined the entire subject of history as an exercise in 'reliving' or 'reconstructing' past lives and thought.[5] This branch of knowledge is known as hermeneutics, or the art of interpretation.[6] However, Collingwood's claim does not in fact apply to all forms of historical studies. Those analysing aggregated long-term trends – such as (say) fluctuations in the price of grain or the growth of the global population – are making statistical calculations rather than 'reliving' past lives.

That said, however, Collingwood's elevation of empathy paid a significant compliment to its role in human thought and therefore in historical studies. The arts of interpretation, when applied with due caution and sensitivity, are thus much used, particularly in application to social, cultural and political history.

11.3 Oral history

Another way of retrieving the thoughts of ordinary people about the past is by asking them directly. For obvious reasons, however, the collection of witness testimonies, known as oral history, is always hurrying against the ravages of time.[7] Today there are no living combat veterans of the First World War who can tell their tales anew. Yet collected interviews, carefully compiled, can fill the void. In the UK, the Imperial War Museum holds some 800,000+ personal testimonies of war and conflicts, covering twentieth-century British and Commonwealth history.[8] And there are similar memory-archives relating to epic contestations such as the 1930s

[4] N. Stargardt, *The German War: a Nation under Arms, 1939–45* (London, 2015).

[5] R. G. Collingwood, *The Idea of History*, ed. T. M. Knox (pub. posthumously, London, 1946).

[6] J. Zimmermann, *Hermeneutics: a Very Short Introduction* (Oxford, 2015); J. D. Caputo, *Hermeneutics: Facts and Interpretation in the Age of Information* (London, 2018); Retz, *Empathy and History.*

[7] Thompson, *Voice of the Past*; D. A. Ritchie, *Doing Oral History: a Practical Guide* (New York, 2015); A. Zusman, *Story Bridges: a Guide for Conducting Intergenerational Oral History Projects* (London, 2016); F.-A. Montoya and B. Allen, *Practising Oral History to Connect University to Community* (London, 2018); and discussion in sect. 1.5.

[8] The Imperial War Museum website gives details: <https://www.iwm.org.uk/collections> [accessed 30 April 2021].

Spanish Civil War;[9] and the Holocaust in 1940s Germany and Central Europe.[10] This material provides subjective but invaluable evidence which is often entirely unavailable from official sources.

Crucial in all oral history interviews is the rule that the interviewer must not lead the interviewee. It's rigging the answer to say to an industrial worker: 'Tell me about the class struggle in your youth'. Instead, questions should be open: 'What did you think about your boss at work?' And, depending upon the answer, this opener might be followed by: 'Would you say that your attitude was generally shared by others who worked with you?' Often, however, people's memories don't fit into neat models of class struggle or any other abstract category. So researchers shouldn't press unduly for details on points that don't get a response but instead proceed to those that do.

Having recorded the interviews, further obvious rules also apply. The primary source for oral history is the audio recording in its original format. It should therefore be preserved, even where a full transcript is available. New tools for the analysis of audio data are emerging all the time – and, at some future date, these sources may be re-analysed in new ways.

When making a transcript of an interview, every word should be recorded verbatim, including all the hesitations and circumlocutions of everyday speech.[11] The witnesses should then be invited to authenticate the record (most readily agree); and, ideally, both the recording and the transcript should be deposited in a relevant archive. If that is not possible, then they should at least be stored in some format that is open to inspection by others.

Public scrutiny of the original record provides the only good guarantee that the first collector has not invented, mangled or quoted material out of context. Once this new-minted historical evidence is publicly available, then it is open to study and interpretation by other researchers too. And they, of course, are equally enjoined not to garble, to cut unfairly or to quote witnesses' words out of context. Original recollections need the same careful evaluation that is given to all historical sources. That is to say, living witnesses have their own subjective viewpoints and axes to grind. But a multitude of sometimes conflicting witnesses provide a spectrum of testimonies for historians to ponder. Oral history is particularly well

---

[9] See JISC (Joint Information Systems Committee) Archives Hub, 'The Spanish Civil War', for source survey: <https://archiveshub.jisc.ac.uk/features/spanishcivilwar.shtml> [accessed 30 April 2021].

[10] There is much key material in many different countries. The British Library's guide provides a fine starting-point: see <https://www.bl.uk/collection-guides/oral-histories-of-jewish-experience-and-holocaust-testimonies> [accessed 30 April 2021].

[11] T. Bergen, *Transcribing Oral History* (London, 2019).

used for recent political and military history, as well as to illuminate many themes in social, cultural and gender history.

11.4 Prosopography, or group biography

Interpreting the past lives of the silent and 'ordinary' people of history, especially in the eras before mass literacy, has triggered a variety of recovery techniques. One methodology which is popular in both historical studies and the social sciences is known as prosopography (a word that many stumble to pronounce!).[12] A simpler term is 'group biography'. By putting many unremarkable life stories together, historians can detect bigger patterns, whether established statistically or in qualitative terms – and this technique also compensates for the fact that many lives are poorly documented. Prosopography contains 'soft' elements of interpretation but it tries to combine them with as much reliable factual data as can be discovered about the people under collective review.

One key originator of this methodology in historical studies was Lewis Namier (born Ludwik Niemirowski), the eminent British historian of Polish/Jewish heritage.[13] Suspicious of grand ideas, he valued instead the stability of structures. In particular, he admired Britain's eighteenth-century Parliament and he revised its political history by looking not at the frontline politicians but the quiet back-benchers instead. His specific conclusions were hotly contested. Yet his method, initially known as 'Namierism', was soon copied by others. Indeed, the History of Parliament Project, which he drove forward in the 1950s, continues to flourish today, providing in-depth biographical surveys of all MPs while also assessing their collective impact.[14]

Among the merits of a prosopographical approach is the quasi-novelistic weaving together of many different life stories. The effect is to curb an over-emphasis upon 'great men (and women)' in favour of ordinary mortals. And this approach encourages historians to take networks, linkages and relationships seriously – all of which are powerful historical forces. Recent developments in 'network theory' and computer-based analysis have generated new enthusiasm for this approach. For example, studies of group

---

[12] K. S. B. Keats-Rohan, *Prosopography Approaches and Applications: a Handbook* (Oxford, 2007).

[13] For L. B. Namier, see L. Colley, *Namier* (London, 1989), and D. Hayton, *Conservative Revolutionary: the Lives of Lewis Namier* (Manchester, 2019).

[14] This project, first mooted in 1928, was activated in 1941 and has been funded since 1951 by the British Treasury: <https://www.historyofparliamentonline.org> [accessed 30 April 2021].

contacts across cultures and through time throw significant light upon the transmission of ideas and the diffusion of cultural values.[15]

Like many techniques, however, prosopography can be overdone if it is taken as the only valid focus. An exaggerated stress upon the structures of groups and networks can seriously underplay the impact of ideas – and leaders – and of long-term underlying forces – and short-term contingencies and accidents. And while computer-generated visualizations of networks are often impressive, they need to do more than simply demonstrate linkages that are already known.

The technique of prosopography thus works best when supported by a sufficient quantity of good, reliable sources. It also needs to be deployed in a suitable analytical context and applied to a historically coherent group. In the right circumstances, however, it can produce from patchy evidence much more than the sum of its component parts. As already noted, prosopography is used productively not only in political and religious history but also in social and cultural history, and in the history of ideas.

11.5 Reading the silences

'Reading the silences', meanwhile, is a counter-technique for interpreting documents against the grain, which is derived from literary and social studies. It corresponds with a current fascination among cultural historians with the history of silence itself.[16] (Unsurprisingly, noise is attracting serious attention too.)[17]

Techniques of 'reading between the lines' direct attention towards what the sources do not say, alongside what they do.[18] It can be applied to spoken words as well as written words. Therapists as well as historians and literary scholars are keenly aware that crucial things may be left unsaid and unwritten. Ambiguities can thrive on nods and winks, without being closely specified.[19]

---

[15] See A. Goldgar, *Impolite Learning: Conduct and Community in the Republic of Letters, 1680–1750* (London, 1995); A. Collar, *Religious Networks in the Roman Empire: the Spread of New Ideas* (New York, 2013); C. Barr and H. M. Carey, *Religion and Greater Ireland: Christianity and Irish Global Networks, 1750–1950* (Montreal, 2015).

[16] A. Corbain, *A History of Silence: From the Renaissance to the Present Day*, transl. J. Birrell (Cambridge, 2018); J. Brox, *Silence: a Social History of One of the Least Understood Elements of Our Lives* (Boston, Mass., 2019).

[17] See P. Hegarty, *Noise/Music: a History* (London, 2007); D. Hendy, *Noise: a Human History of Sound and Listening* (London, 2013); and song history, as in Palmer, *The Sound of History*.

[18] R. Batchelor, *Interpreting Silence* (Victoria, BC, 1994).

[19] See the classic study by W. Empson, *Seven Types of Ambiguity* (London, 1930); and also E. Williams, *Reading Beyond the Lines: Exercises in Inferential Comprehension* (London, 1978).

Sometimes, indeed, major issues are deliberately kept secret. It can therefore be very liberating for oppressed individuals – and educational for society at large – to unlock the 'silenced voices'. For example, communities which have traditionally avoided personal confessions about sexual matters can find it cathartic (as well as shocking) to acknowledge sexual diversity or to reveal direct experiences of sexual abuse. Notable historical examples include studies of the war-time exploitation of the so-called comfort women in the Far East. This research has broken taboos to add significantly to knowledge and also to prompt calls for sincere retrospective recognition/contrition.[20]

With the active use of empathy and group biographies, 'reading the silences' within the archives can also be another way of addressing the well-known biases in many official, and indeed unofficial, source collections. As already noted, historians know of the past existence of innumerable populations – working people, the enslaved, the illiterate, the disabled – whose lives and views are very difficult to recover. Even when they do appear in reports, the accounts may be hostile or uncomprehending. Hence identifying significant gaps in the historical record – listening to the archival silences – offers one way of recovering the experiences of such groups.[21] It's a way of letting past themes lead the research rather than simply relying upon surviving evidence.

However, the process of silence-reading requires great care, especially when applied after a significant lapse of time. Assumptions and evidence need to be clarified, and allowance made for alternative interpretations. There remains a risk that later readers may project their own concerns into gaps in earlier sources, without appreciating how both languages and the conventions of communication have changed.[22]

There's also a related danger that later generations may be encouraged to castigate people from the past for not having said or written what later generations want them to have said or written. Such moves risk turning history into an exercise in anachronistic blame-games. So silences need to be analysed with great sensitivity to context – and the resulting interpretation supported by corroborative evidence, if at all possible. The technique, often used in literary studies,[23] can also be applied to the history of ideas and

---

[20] S. J. Friedman, *Silenced No More: Voices of Comfort Women* (Hong Kong, 2015); and debates about the aftermath in J. E. Stromseth (ed.), *Accountability for Atrocities: National and International Responses* (Ardsley, N.Y., 2003).

[21] For an excellent example, see Fuentes, *Dispossessed Lives*.

[22] See assessment in B. Poland and A. Pederson, 'Reading between the lines: interpreting silences in qualitative research', *Qualitative Research*, iv (1998), 293–312.

[23] L. Brosnan, *Reading Virginia Woolf's Essays and Journalism: Breaking the Surface of Silence* (Edinburgh, 1997).

cultural attitudes. And it's especially relevant when exploring all taboo issues, such as the difficult history of human abuse of other humans.[24]

11.6 'Thick' cultural description

'Thick' description is intended to signify 'richly textured', although unfortunately the adjective can imply something less flattering like 'obtuse' or 'dense'. The concept came initially from the British philosopher Gilbert Ryle. He contrasted 'thin' surface observations with 'thick' contextual descriptions, as rival forms of analysis.[25] The usage was then propelled into global circulation by the US anthropologist Clifford Geertz. He delighted in 'thickness' as a way of interpreting everyday events within the web of social and cultural meanings which they held for the people involved.[26] This approach entails treating all communities with equal respect, on their own terms. It immediately resonated with anthropologically minded historians. One such was E. P. Thompson, who specifically sought, when writing British working-class history, to avoid the 'enormous condescension of posterity'.[27] His dictum has been widely quoted, as it indicated the need for cultural humility. Other societies in other times – and other social classes – were not to be dismissed by historians as 'primitive', 'savage' or 'backward'.

Bolstered by such credentials, a number of excellent in-depth social and cultural histories promptly followed. Celebrated examples included LeRoy Ladurie's *Montaillou* (1975), which explored the lifestyles and beliefs of the early fourteenth-century inhabitants of a small village in the Pyrenees.[28] This study contributed to 'history from below' with the aid of a surviving cache of detailed Inquisition records. Its runaway success in fact encouraged a relative intellectual shift, within the French *Annales* school of historians[29]

[24] For another case-history, see S. Kalayci, *Reading Silences: Essays on Women, Memory and War in Twentieth-Century Turkey* (London, 2021); and for the domestic context, see N. A. Jackson (ed.), *Encyclopaedia of Domestic Violence* (London, 2007).

[25] G. Ryle (1900–76), *On Thinking* (London, 1979).

[26] C. Geertz, 'Thick description: towards an interpretive theory of culture', in Geertz, *The Interpretation of Cultures: Selected Essays* (New York, 1973), pp. 3–30. See also D. N. McCloskey, 'Thick and thin methodologies in the history of economic thought', in *The Popperian Legacy in Economics*, ed. N. de Marchi (Cambridge, 1988), pp. 245–58.

[27] Thompson, *Making of English Working Class* (1968 edn), p. 12.

[28] E. LeRoy Ladurie, *Montaillou: Cathars and Catholics in a French Village, 1294–1324*, transl. B. Bray (London, 1978).

[29] P. Burke, *The French Historical Revolution: the Annales School, 1929–89* (Cambridge, 1990); A. Burguière, *The Annales School: an Intellectual History*, transl. J. M. Todd (Ithaca, N.Y., 2009); and criticisms explored in J. Tendler, *Opponents of the Annales School* (Basingstoke, 2013).

and elsewhere, towards in-depth studies of 'mentalities', and away from analyses of long-term trends. It was a powerful monument to 'synchronic immersion' (sinking deeply into one moment from the past).

Indeed, some enthusiasts urge that the whole approach constitutes a new 'interpretive turn' in the making of knowledge.[30] But criticisms have also followed. *Montaillou* specifically was challenged as to how far the Inquisitorial records, written retrospectively, really provided reliable evidence of the inner beliefs of villagers who were summoned to testify.[31] More generally, too, critics wonder how far the subsequent cultural interpreters were moulding the evidence to fit their own views, perhaps subconsciously.

Eventually, there was a risk of diminishing returns. How many affectionately detailed probes of specific populations at specific times are needed? What can 'thick' accounts convey, without some understanding of wider trends in play? Here, familiar tensions arise between short- and long-term histories; and between local and global views.

Taking the example of the Second World War again, a 'thick' description of life within Hitler's Berlin bunker, exploring the mental world of Hitler and his closest supporters, has undoubted analytical value. Moreover, it's a serious interpretative challenge to understand the Nazi viewpoint, without sharing or endorsing it.[32] Yet the experiences of Hitler and his closest companions were but part of a global war, which also needs global analysis.

'Thick' cultural description thus best conveys an informative part of the whole, rather than an entire history, complete with trends over time. It is deployed most frequently in social and cultural history and in some political/cultural studies.

Since Geertz's first intervention, there have been various other claimed 'turns' in styles of analysis.[33] One example stands proxy for many. Thus the

---

[30] D. R. Hiley et al. (ed.), *The Interpretive Turn: Philosophy, Science, Culture* (Ithaca, N.Y., 1991); D. Bachmann-Medick, *Cultural Turns: New Orientations in the Study of Culture* (London, 2016). Note on terminology: American English prefers the elided form of 'interpretive', while British English commonly sticks to 'interpretative', except in this particular context.

[31] C. Hay, 'Review of Montaillou', *Oral History*, vii (1979), 70–1.

[32] J. Fest, *Inside Hitler's Bunker: the Last Ten Days of the Third Reich*, transl. M. B. Dembo (London, 2004); S. F. Kellerhoff, *The Führer Bunker: Hitler's Last Refuge* (Berlin, 2004).

[33] S. Susen, *The Postmodern Turn in the Social Sciences* (Basingstoke, 2015); H. Marsh, *The Comic Turn in Contemporary English Fiction: Who's Laughing Now?* (London, 2020); G. Dürbeck and P. Hüpkes (ed.), *The Anthropocentric Turn: the Interplay between Disciplinary and Interdisciplinary Responses to a New Age* (London, 2020); L. Moyo, *The Decolonial Turn in Africa and the Global South* (London, 2020).

'material turn' (2010) entails a close study of historical artefacts and brings fresh perspectives from unexpected sources.[34] This subsequent diversification has taken some of the initial glamour away from 'thick' description. Yet the approach has intellectual value – and also attracts curious readers – so it will undoubtedly remain a welcome part of the historian's armoury.

11.7 What ifs? Or, counterfactual history

Counterfactual history (also known as 'virtual' history) always remains conjectural and hence controversial. It goes in and out of fashion.[35] In many ways, that fate is hardly surprising. It's hard enough to establish an authoritative history based upon accurate data, without wishing to think 'counter' to the facts.

Nevertheless, it's worth reviewing the pros and cons of studying What Ifs?, since humans do think in terms of options, both when planning ahead and when assessing the past.

Such observations can also contribute to the search for so-called hinge factors in history: specific actions or non-actions which at times triggered key turning-points.[36] With reference to the Second World War, for example, it might well be argued that: *Hitler's greatest mistake was to invade Russia in June 1941.* The implication-against-the-facts would follow that: *had he not done so, the outcome of the war would have been different* – or even that: *Germany may not have lost.* However, while it is easy to note the importance of Hitler's decision, it is impossible to prove an alternative scenario. Often, conclusions are trite: *things would have been quite otherwise.* (Or cautious: *the prevailing trends were such that, even with different decisions, things would have remained broadly the same.*)

Moreover, the wider the scope of the counterfactual speculation, the more difficult it becomes to define an answer. *What if European travellers had not sailed to North America in the fifteenth century? What if the French Revolution never happened?* When one big variable changes, then very many others are highly likely to adapt also. So the answer to the above questions is really: *Who can say?*

---

[34] T. Bennett and P. Joyce (ed.), *Material Powers: Cultural Studies, History and the Material Turn* (Cham, 2010).

[35] See N. Ferguson (ed.), *Virtual History: Alternatives and Counterfactuals* (London, 1997; New York, 1999); J. Black, *What If? Counterfactualism and the Problem of History* (London, 2008); C. Gallagher, *Telling It Like It Wasn't: the Counterfactual Imagination in History and Fiction* (Chicago, Ill., 2018).

[36] E. Durschmied, *The Hinge Factor: How Chance and Stupidity Have Changed History* (London, 1999); A. Axelrod, *100 Turning Points in Military History* (London, 2019).

For a while in the 1960s and 1970s, there was a fashion for counterfactual calculations to be undertaken by quantitative methods. Economic historians created a statistical mode of a given economy and then reran the model minus one key variable. Robert Fogel's study of nineteenth-century American growth without the railways was a paradigmatic case.[37] His conclusion was counter-intuitive. The railways were allegedly not as important to the USA's economic and political development as is generally assumed. Yet, as critics noted, if one factor is changed retrospectively, then it's likely that others would be transformed too. No steam trains would presumably mean no steam power. So the basic structure of the economy – and hence its statistical modelling – would have needed a major rejig.[38] Would the Americans have invented some other technology instead? Or would their economy have remained wind-, water- and horse-powered? Again, the answer remains: *Who can say with any certainty?*

Pursuing 'virtual' speculations too far results in non-histories, which are beyond proof or disproof. Nonetheless, it is important for historians to be aware of this approach; and to be ready to challenge any overly dogmatic counterfactual assertions.

Furthermore, imagining the unknown is a theme of historical value in its own right. It is intriguing to review past speculations about alternative outcomes. These imagined possibilities could have at times a genuine polemical or visionary force.[39] In sum, counterfactual considerations are part of history. They can also remain relevant for historians when debating the impact of key decisions – for example, in political or military strategy. It remains the case, however, that these *What if?* speculations remain subjective assessments or calculations. However entertaining – or annoying – they may be, they do not constitute authoritative explanations of the unfolding past.[40]

11.8 Summary: 'soft' approaches, not soppy outcomes

All 'soft' techniques of interpretation have great value, when used appropriately. They do begin to lose their heft if their claims are overdone, but that applies to all methodologies.

---

[37] R. W. Fogel, *Railroads and American Economic Growth: Essays in Econometric History* (Baltimore, Md., 1964, 1970).

[38] P. D. McClelland, 'Railroads, American growth and the new economic history: a critique', *Journal of Economic History*, xxviii (1968), 102–23.

[39] J. McTague, *Things That Didn't Happen: Writing, Politics and the Counterhistorical, 1678–1743* (Woodbridge, 2019).

[40] For a robust critique, see R. J. Evans, *Altered Pasts: Counterfactuals in History* (London, 2014).

These 'soft' approaches are used to tackle immensely difficult and contentious historical themes, as shown by some of the examples cited in this chapter. When done well – with clearly explained methods and assumptions – they produce tough, important and validated conclusions, not soppy, irrelevant and sentimental outcomes.

Overall, qualitative assessments should really be renamed less pejoratively – or, conversely, the adjective 'soft' should get a better reputation. The art of interpretation is an intrinsic part of historical analysis. Qualitative and quantitative approaches are thus not rival but complementary modes of thought.

12. Troubleshooting

SIGNPOST: Chiefly aimed at those researching within educational institutions, but also contains advice for freelance researchers on avoiding intellectual isolation and finding friendly mentors. The final sections on promoting a culture that avoids bullying and harassment are applicable to all scholars across the board.

In tribute to helping hands.

12.1 Working in partnership

Working in partnership to generate new historical knowledge is usually an exciting and fulfilling experience for supervisors and researchers alike. Often close friendships are generated which last a lifetime.

On the other hand, sometimes (relatively rarely) the relationships can go wrong and become unproductive. That's a real shame, but should not be allowed to develop into a catastrophe. The best advice for all parties, when becoming aware that things are going wrong, is to behave calmly and professionally. And to involve a third party, who can intervene to break the deadlock. So asking for help is a positive first step. Seeking practical alternatives turns a potential melodrama into an organizational reshuffle, which is near to routine.

In the 'bad old days' (in this context up until the 1980s), supervisors were very hit-and-miss. A number of them were marvellously stimulating. Another number were utterly negligent. And many were in between, not giving much supervision, chiefly because most of them had not been closely supervised themselves. In caricature, the learned don would offer a glass of sherry to the neophyte; murmur a word of encouragement; and direct the student to the nearest archive. If, after a period of ten years or so, the self-motivated researcher emerged with a thesis, everyone would be pleased. (This account is a caricature, but only just.) However, those days have truly gone. Most supervisors now supervise pro-actively; all departments and faculties provide clear frameworks for the process; and students have much higher expectations. Hence, if things go less than well, there are mechanisms in place which will help to find solutions.

12.2 Resolving general problems of supervision

To be sure, problems of supervision can initially loom large. Postgraduates, as the junior partners in the relationship, often feel anxious and intimidated. There are unruly human emotions involved. And there are grey areas, where supervisors' attempts at encouragement may spill over into bullying, even if not intended as such. And there are other potential sources of postgraduate 'blues'. These may include writer's block (discussed in chapter 9); intellectual loneliness; worries about future job prospects; and, possibly, stress from intentional bullying or harassment (see section 12.3).

However, there is no point in struggling on in silence. And still less point in dropping out in despair. That outcome used to be more common. Today, by contrast, all parties realize how detrimental it was, to the research process, to the well-being of individual researchers, and to the reputation of the department or faculty. Institutions are judged on completion rates, so having effective systems of supervision and review is essential. Therefore problems can be raised in a calm and professional manner, expecting a calm and professional response.

As already noted, departments and faculties already institute regular reviews of progress and they require that each session of supervision is formally recorded. Such systems are explicitly designed to pick up any problems and to find solutions. It's generally rare to find a state of postgraduate blues which cannot be alleviated.

Incidentally, a new communications hazard has emerged with the advent of social media. People can take to the airwaves too rapidly for considered judgement; and they can share too much. Since academics should try to write coolly, rather than in a polemical frenzy, it's not a good idea for any party to fire off hostile or combative messages on social media (see fuller discussion in chapter 8).

Very much the same advice applies to freelance historians working outside the academic world. Much the most frequent problem confronting people carrying out research without an institutional framework of support is intellectual loneliness. It's good therefore to enlist a few friends who will act as informal mentors. Getting someone to listen sympathetically to problems and perhaps to read some chapters can be truly helpful, even if the friends have no special expertise in the field.

Another variant of that tactic is to join a discussion or reading group with others who share similar interests. Contact with others breaks down feelings of isolation and can often provide a first step to finding solutions. As in the case of unblocking writer's block (see chapter 9), the art of coping sensibly with difficulties can be made into a positive learning experience.

12.3 Resolving problems of bullying and harassment

Most workplaces have comprehensive policies which address problems of bullying and sexual harassment. In educational institutions, both forms of behaviour are banned outright. A complete interdiction includes all sexual relationships between staff and students.[1] And the ban applies even in cases where mutual agreement might be forthcoming. Love affairs should also be put on hold for the duration of a professional relationship. The inherent inequality of power and status between academics and students means that consent between equals is deemed impossible. Similarly, the disparity in institutional roles means that the potential for bullying is always present.

Such rules contribute to the continuing challenge within wider society as well as within the education system to subdue interpersonal aggression and to entrench socially acceptable and non-coercive codes of sexual relationships.[2] The universities have long known that putting bright, admiring apprentice scholars with bright, admirable academics, as many are, can generate intense relationships. Indeed, the whole process of one-on-one supervision is

---

[1] There are some well-known cases of happy marriages between teachers and their former students (one being that of President Macron of France, whose wife taught him French and Latin when he was at high school), but convention today requires that romantic and sexual relationships be postponed until the pedagogic relationship is ended.

[2] For long-term trends – not without controversy – see J. Weeks, *Sex, Politics and Society: the Regulation of Sexuality since 1800* (Abingdon, 2017); S. Pinker, *The Better Angels of Our Nature: the Decline of Violence in History and Its Causes* (London, 2011).

designed to generate a kind of intellectual intimacy; and that closeness can tend to develop into other varieties. Having a crush on one's best teacher is a common, if often fleeting, educational experience. And academics may equally get caught up in their own maelstrom of emotions, with the wide-eyed admiration from apprentice scholars making up for any other problems in the wider world.[3]

For many years, considerable latitude was tacitly allowed to senior figures (usually powerful men). Illicit affairs and bullying featured regularly in campus plays and novels.[4] Willy Russell's wry drama, *Educating Rita* (1981), and David Mamet's darker *Oleanna* (1992) explored implicit and explicit sexual tensions between the teacher and the taught.[5] Alison Lurie's witty *War between the Tates* (1974) also extracted humour and social observation from illicit campus entanglements. Meanwhile, Malcolm Bradbury's *The History Man* (1975) featured both bullying and wily sexual intrigues. The novel's main protagonist, the academic Howard Kirk, saw himself as a left-leaning progressive figure, encapsulating the trend of the times. Hence he was the 'history man'. Yet he is a deeply manipulative figure. Bradbury seems to half-admire his resourceful anti-hero. In all, however, the novel satirizes male power politics and sexual entitlement – even among 'right-on', trendy left-wingers.

Moreover, bullying and sexual harassment spread doubt and disillusionment throughout the wider community. Would-be secret affairs rarely remain completely secret for long. At one point in Bradbury's novel, Howard Kirk remarks that: 'Most beds aren't as intimate as people think they are'.[6] It was a telling point. Staff–student affairs – or even rumours of the same – generate pervasive jealousies, resentment and accusations of favouritism.

Today, however, the framework is shifting, even while problems can and undoubtedly still do occur. These issues are no longer shrouded in silence.

---

[3] Among a growing literature, see B. W. Dziech and L. Weiner, *The Lecherous Professor: Sexual Harassment on Campus* (Boston, Mass., 1984); A. C. Saguy, *What Is Sexual Harassment? From Capitol Hill to the Sorbonne* (London, 2003); C. A. Paludi and M. Paludi (ed.), *Academic and Workplace Sexual Harassment: a Handbook* (London, 2003); and R. Refinetti, *Sexual Harassment and Sexual Consent* (London, 2018).

[4] D. Fuchs and W. Klepuszewski (ed.), *The Campus Novel: Regional or Global?* (Leiden, 2019).

[5] Compare W. Russell, *Educating Rita: a Comedy* (London, 1981), on stage (1980) and film, dir. L. Gilbert (1983); with D. Mamet, *Oleanna*, on stage (1992), on film, dir. D. Mamet (1994), and in print, ed. D. Rosenthal (London, 2004).

[6] M. Bradbury, *The History Man* (London, 1975, 1977), p. 171.

Apprentice scholars expect their mentors to behave with dignity and self-restraint; and equally expect to have access to sympathetic support and remedial action, if needed.

Over the long term, the power imbalance within higher education, while still apparent, has shifted somewhat. Senior 'dons' may have institutional, intellectual and personal kudos. On the other hand, most academics entirely lack the glamour, wealth and power of (say) successful media moguls, film stars, TV personalities, pop stars, glitzy financiers, business tycoons and (even) politicians. Furthermore, the sociological profile of the professoriat is becoming much more variegated, no longer dominated by white heterosexual males. Practically, too, educational administration has become much more bureaucratized. Students' examination grades, prizes and subsequent appointments are awarded by boards and panels, and vetted by committees, rather than by autocratic professors, acting in isolation.

The outcome is a shifting world, where people need to think carefully about their behaviour. Apprentice scholars may also be at fault. Stalking is a complex and destructive phenomenon;[7] and there have been cases of students stalking professors. Nor is that all. There are instances of harassment, bullying, violence and sexual coercion between fellow students, generating another set of difficulties. At best, these are fundamental issues in need of pre-emptive education, assisted by good management and trusted mechanisms for resolving problems. At their most intractable, however, they are matters for the law.

12.4 Ethical safeguards

Codes of good practice can't regulate every permutation in polymorphous human behaviour. Instead, they establish expected norms, which are built into bureaucratic rules. If things go wrong, institutions have mechanisms for reporting complaints. These systems are designed to provide a fair, robust and independent procedure for investigating and dealing with all such cases, bearing in mind (as in any legal system) the possibility of false accusations. In the event of a complaint, it's helpful to have good evidence (such as notes of key meetings), and to present it in a calm and factual manner. Bullying and harassment are highly emotive subjects. And evidence is the best foundation for complaint – and, conversely, the best antidote to false accusation.

---

[7] J. A. Davis (ed.), *Stalking Crimes and Victim Protection: Prevention, Intervention, Threat Assessment and Case Management* (Boca Raton, Fla., 2001); O. Chan and L. L. Sheridan, *Stalking: an International Perspective* (Hoboken, N.J., 2020).

One crucial rule is that no academics should be put into positions that enable them potentially to abuse their power in relation to marking and assessment. Otherwise, there is a risk that confidence in the system could be undermined. At the undergraduate, and MA/MSc level, there are safeguarding processes of double-marking, which are adjudicated by an external examiner and the examination board. At the doctoral level, there is a carefully chosen panel of experts in the field, usually with at least one from an outside institution or department. And then the final award is made by the university's examination board, based upon these examiners' reports. Academic success and all forms of research evaluation should depend upon merit, and merit alone. And be understood as such.

All parties should seek to inculcate a supportive but non-sexualized, non-bullying, non-prejudiced, anti-discriminatory and cooperative work environment.[8] Behaviour that contradicts that aim is morally wrong, often legally prohibited and harmful both academically and personally. As the world of learning is gradually being expanded and democratized around the world, so the entrenching of improved codes of interpersonal behaviour has to be a big part of the process. These are matters of concern for everyone, and future generations of historians will look back with close attention to check how well (or otherwise) the research communities of today have managed.

12.5 Summary: the pleasures of intellectual companionship

Close intellectual companionship is exciting. The pleasures of shared debates and research endeavour can be intense and mentally electrifying. And many of the most rewarding aspects of advanced historical research are found in the informal exchanges and social interactions that are integral to the process.

Lengthy discussions over coffee or in the bar – which may continue late into the evening – are part of the magic of intellectual companionship. And not without reason. It's useful, when mulling over complex ideas, to have a chance to talk them through in depth, with an advisor who is both critic and guide. A good intellectual prod in the right manner and at the right moment can help to hone existing ideas and generate new ones.

Nonetheless, such togetherness should be enjoyed without getting side-tracked into unprofessional behaviour. Academic relationships between

---

[8] D. C. England, *The Essential Guide to Handling Workplace Harassment and Discrimination* (Beverley, Calif., 2018); N. Thompson, *Tackling Bullying and Harassment in the Workplace: a Learning and Development Manual* (Lyme Regis, 2009).

supervisors and researchers – or private sessions between mentors and freelance authors – are based upon imbalances of power and experience. Yet the positive footing of shared commitment can, with sense and goodwill in a non-coercive environment, turn what might be purely routine exchanges into fizzing intellectual firepower.

PART III
Presenting, completing and moving onwards

13. The art of public presentation

SIGNPOST: Relevant to all researchers

Saluting the art of communication.

13.1 Communicating knowledge

The art of public presentation in the academic world and well beyond has improved considerably in recent years. Dotty professors, who could not tell the time of day, are seriously out of fashion. These days, lively engagement and professional presentation have come to be expected.

All speakers recognize the need to communicate knowledge effectively. Explaining the fruits of historical research is not only a socio-cultural good in its own right but is also a great means of clarifying one's thoughts and getting productive feedback. Indeed, in this era of ever-expanding mass communication, the role of public presentations is ever-rising in importance in the historian's range of routine tasks. (See also chapter 8 on social media.)

As a consequence, there is now a goodly literature of advice, both online and in print, with many practical suggestions.[1]

Talking about historical knowledge to a live audience is putting thought 'into action'. And today's audiences participate warmly. There is a positive boom in public demand for historical talks – and new degrees in public history have been crafted to cater for an apparently insatiable interest.[2]

At an earlier stage, in the 1960s and 1970s, there was a cultural pretence that lectures were always boring and had at best to be endured. Speakers would make facetious remarks like: 'Of course, we'd all rather be in the pub'. But such would-be matey comments are annoying and suggest a lack of confidence. Today's audiences, both at public lectures and academic seminars, have opted in and made an effort to attend. If they really want to be in the pub, they probably will be. If not, however, they want and deserve the speaker's best efforts.

By way of encouragement to individual presenters to find their own preferred personal styles, the following sections offer friendly advice, culled from experience.

13.2 Preparing

It's vital, as a starting-point, to check the scheduled timing for every presentation and then make every effort to stick to it. Sometimes it happens that there has been a change of plans – or perhaps one speaker on a panel has overrun. In such cases, chairs these days are usually firm and call the proceedings to a close. If that happens, speakers should not attempt to gabble the remainder of their talk at high speed. Much the best advice is to switch immediately, and with good grace, into a short conclusion. At least that way, the audience is left with the main message.

Another starting-point is to check out the room layout in advance. It's good to look quickly for oneself (whether virtually or in person), or to get a brief description from the event organizer. Having a sense of the room dynamics allows for excellent subliminal preparation.

Similarly, it's also wise to ask in advance about the available technology. It's pointless arriving to lecture with PowerPoint if there's no suitable screen. These days, organizers are usually good at advance preparation; and they

[1] J. Rendle-Short, *The Academic Presentation: Situated Talk in Action* (London, 2016).
[2] For debates, see A. Curthoys and P. Hamilton, 'What makes history public?' *Public History Review*, i (1992), 8–13; P. Ashton and H. Kean (ed.), *People and Their Pasts: Public History Today* (Basingstoke, 2009); J. B. Gardner and P. Hamilton (ed.), *The Oxford Handbook of Public History* (New York, 2017); P. Ashton and A. Trapeznik (ed.), *What Is Public History Globally? Working with the Past in the Present* (London, 2019).

expect guest speakers to be well prepared likewise. Hence it goes without saying that it's essential to learn how to operate PowerPoint before the talk, rather than during it.

Particularly important also as advance preparation is to check the academic level at which the presentation should be pitched and to organize the material accordingly. So an audience of newcomers to the subject needs a good general introduction and key definitions before getting into the detail. But, with experts, it's good to aim high. They quickly become bored if told at length about things they already know well.

A mixed audience of experts and non-experts is the most difficult to handle. It's useful to cover key definitions, or otherwise those not familiar with the material will be stranded. So it's a good challenge to present the basics in a sharp and interesting way, to keep the experts happy. Then phrases like 'let's just recapitulate for those unfamiliar with the material' help to reassure those who already know the subject well that they are not being underestimated. It's a question of tone. By the way, the advance preparation should always include lightly revising the material if it has already been given before. Each presentation should be delivered as freshly minted.

13.3 Style of delivery

Fortunately, the human voice is a tremendous instrument for communication. Speakers should take encouragement from that – and find their own personal style within the spectrum. A variety of tone and pitch is always helpful. By contrast, a droning monotone will numb listeners' brains. In addition, a variety of gestures and terminology adds colour and excitement. Live speakers can also make good use of the occasional significant strategic pause. (But not on radio, as producers detest a blank silence.)

As a general rule, clear and expressive voices appeal to audiences. Moreover, a special slow diction, clearly but not mechanically demarcating one word from another, is good to cultivate for lectures to polyglot international audiences with very diverse levels of linguistic attainment.

Standing to lecture or to give a seminar presentation is generally more successful than sitting. Audiences can see and respond better and vice versa. Sometimes a panel of speakers will be seated at a table together. It's still good advice to stand up when invited to speak, even if the others don't. Standing allows speakers to use the diaphragm to control the volume and timbre of speech more easily. Walking around the stage is also fine, if it comes naturally. But the wandering should be kept under control, and should be avoided altogether if a session is being filmed. Speakers have been known to patrol the aisles of the hall, or even to dive under a desk. Such manoeuvres make amusing talking points afterwards but, at the time, audiences often feel, uncomfortably, that the speaker has ceased to concentrate on them.

Expressive body language is eminently helpful, including appropriate hand gestures; but not to the point of distracting audiences from the message. 'Historian's hands' – waving wildly to emphasize a point – should be avoided, especially on TV.

Those new to academic presentation generally prefer to start with a fully written text. That's understandable, since quotations have to be accurate, and the sequence of points made clear. A formal text can also be revised for publication or inclusion in a thesis. However, it's vital to keep the voice very expressive – and the pace varied. Some presenters manage to craft their texts into their own natural 'speaking' style. Others start by incorporating chunks of free speech into the presentation. Experienced lecturers can manage entirely from notes. It's a technique that can be learned incrementally. Thus it's easy enough to look up and speak directly to the audience when switching from one section of an argument to the next. Even a short break from reading from a prepared text renders the voice more natural – and keeps the audience on its mental toes. Then over time, the amount of free speaking can be expanded. But there's no absolute rule. Speakers should find a style with which they feel confident and at ease.

Looking up from a written text enables those who are really intent upon communication to undertake another key manoeuvre. It entails from time to time moving one's gaze slowly and deliberately around the room. That ecumenical signal indicates a desire to communicate with all – and not just to talk to the front row of the audience – or to the speaker's shoes. This circulating gaze is like a 'lighthouse beam'. Of course, it must not turn into a rude or pointed stare. But the round-room gaze is an excellent way of 'collecting' a roomful of disparate people into one meeting. It underlines the unspoken compact of reciprocity between speakers and audiences.

In all circumstances, it's best to appear smiling and affable. Even speakers who are having a bad day should put aside their woes and focus cheerfully upon the audience, who will immediately respond. It's fine to use humour when appropriate. Shared laughter bonds groups together. But there is no need to force matters if the subject under discussion (such as trends in the price of grain) is not a natural rib-tickler. It's enough to radiate good cheer. By the way, it hardly needs saying that speakers should not pre-fortify their courage with alcohol. That tactic doesn't work. Alcohol promotes incoherence and a false *bonhomie*, causing speakers to perform worse while thinking that they are doing better. Sober goodwill and smiles will more than suffice.

13.4 *Structuring contents*

At the very start of a presentation, it's an excellent idea for the speaker to gaze lightly round the entire room and then deliver an opening salvo with great conviction. Attention is immediately caught, and a sense of excitement communicated. Audiences like an element of performance, although they do want a presentation to have scintillating contents too. By contrast, it's uninspiring when speakers start by mumbling: 'Um, err, thank you for inviting me to talk'. Or 'How do I operate the PowerPoint?' Or even 'Can you hear me at the back?' (Both speakers and organizers should have checked the acoustics beforehand.) Even worse are half-hearted apologies: 'I'm sorry that it's so cold this evening/that you've had to come out in the rain/that you're missing a great TV programme' … or whatever. Disastrous.

Then, after a smart start, it's helpful for speakers to explain briefly the structure of the talk that is to follow. Providing such a framework is one of the most important arts of public presentation – and too often the most unduly neglected. Clear structures indicate that speakers are well prepared. They also allow audiences to follow the train of thought and simultaneously to understand how the details fit into a bigger argument. Not only are hour-long presentations greatly improved by clear structures, but so too are even short five-minute interventions. It's always possible to announce something like: 'I have three points to make' or 'four examples to give' or 'five errors to denounce' or whatever. Then, as the talk unfolds (whether at length or briefly), speakers can indicate when they are moving from one section to the next.

Such frameworks assist those in the audience who are taking notes, and they encourage all to remember key points. By contrast, an unstructured stream-of-consciousness presentation may start well but quickly sags – and is very hard to summarize afterwards.

How the contents of a presentation are organized will vary according to the material in hand. A list of numbered headings will suffice. Or the points can be grouped to advance an argument. One classic option is to adopt a binary division: 'on the one hand' … 'on the other'. That structure enables a legal case to test systematically the prosecution against the defence.[3] It works well when there are two clearly opposing viewpoints.

Yet it's not helpful to cram complex discussions into binary divisions that don't do justice to the issues. So three-part arguments constitute another often-favoured option. Three headings provide scope for complexity (not

---

[3] M. Pirie, *How to Win Every Argument: the Use and Abuse of Logic* (London, 2015); W. Huhn, *The Five Types of Legal Argument* (Durham, N.C., 2014).

everything is either black or white), while still offering a manageable structure that audiences can recollect. *This* viewpoint is contrasted with *that* viewpoint, while both are compared with a third, which may contain elements of both.

However, flexibility and clarity are the key requirements. There's no need to follow a pre-set pattern. Speakers should organize their material as best helps an argument to unfold – and signal the chosen route to the audience.[4]

While unfolding an argument, it's important to keep track of time. One useful tip is to insert timings into the text or notes. It is okay to digress briefly at various points, particularly when following a new train of thought which has been triggered by free-style speaking. But it's essential not to let a bright digression take over the entire talk. Hence, if following a new strand of ideas, it's good to ensure that the audience knows that the argument is going into a relevant by-way – and that it knows too when the main route has been resumed. Speakers and audiences are sharing the journey together.

13.5 The sense of an ending

Endings of spoken presentations should be strong, clear and memorable, as already recommended for written work (see section 7.7). These days, there is a folksy style abroad in both politics and academic life that concludes very simply, by thanking the audience for listening. That tactic has one advantage, in that it signals to the audience that it's time to clap. Yet the formula is weak and uninspiring. Much better to sign off with something not meek but memorable.

Conclusions to academic presentations certainly should not come as bolts from the blue. Instead, they offer summations of the accumulating verdict to which the entire presentation has been leading.[5] Precisely how the last words are fashioned is a matter of personal choice – and will depend also upon the nature of the material. At times, a considered statement will be appropriate. At other times, a snappy dictum. Nonetheless, whatever the format, the finale should be delivered with the same force and intensity as the opening.

Without asserting dogmatically that a short summary statement (the 'snappy dictum') should always be used, it's worth noting that a brief but telling summary can be particularly useful at the end of a live talk. It encapsulates the argument. It provides the audience with a memorable

[4] There are many studies of the art of rhetoric, from Aristotle onwards: see S. J. Coopman and J. Lull, *Public Speaking: the Evolving Art* (London, 2012).
[5] See, classically, F. Kermode, *The Sense of an Ending: Studies in the Theory of Fiction with a New Epilogue* (London, 1967; Oxford, 2000).

finale. And it shows that the speakers have managed successfully to distil their complex thoughts into a format akin to an aphorism or an epigram, of up to (say) ten words. That ability is itself a valuable one. Indeed, the art of summarizing pithily is as challenging in its way as is the art of expounding lengthily.

Interestingly, too, this skill is not a recent invention. Classical Latin was capable of being used with admirable brevity. Many choice phrases survive, not just in heraldry but also in everyday exchanges:[6] 'Caveat emptor' (Let the buyer beware); 'Nil Desperandum' (Never despair); 'Carpe diem' (Seize the day/enjoy life while you can).

Moreover, since 2006, the skill of brevity has become immensely popularized by the successful social networking service known as Twitter – now matched by a host of parallel systems (see chapter 8). This format allows users to communicate in snappy posts of not more than 240 characters including spaces. The impact of this terse style is already great and (in 2021) still unfolding.[7]

Whether the skills of laconic brevity are satisfactory in public life when divorced from the skills of in-depth analysis is becoming an urgent political as much as socio-cultural question for the twenty-first century.

Yet, for academic communicators, it remains good – although not imperative – to round out an impressive exposition with a memorable ending. And, of course, the better the content of the prior analysis, the more definitive the concluding dictum or statement will be.

13.6 Summary: using the opportunity

Researchers should always welcome the chance to convey their research to the wider world. Meanings are often made in the course of communicating, and messages clarified by the exercise. All the above advice about preparation, lecturing style and structured contents applies equally when apprentice historians launch into their first teaching of undergraduates.

Summarizing advanced research for non-experts is a great challenge, as is answering the questions of keen and critical student audiences, or engaging the less critical ones. It is truly rare that the subject fails to excite interest.

---

[6] E. Ehrlich, *A Dictionary of Latin Tags and Phrases* (London, 1987); J. Parker, *Living Latin: the Heritage of Latin Phrases and Quotations in English* (Portlaoise, Ireland, 2016).

[7] For debates, see Z. Tufekci, *Twitter and Teargas: the Power and Fragility of Networked Protest* (New Haven, Conn., 2017); V. Forrestal and T. Vella, *Using Twitter to Build Communities: a Primer for Libraries, Archives and Museums* (Lanham, Md., 2018); but see also C. Fuchs, *Digital Demagogue: Authoritarian Capitalism in the Age of Trump and Twitter* (London, 2018).

History is human and therefore ... hot! So here's a summary twelve-word dictum for all speakers: *Sharing history with attentive audiences is a privilege – so use it well!*

13.7 Coda: a historic example of a bad paper, and a great response (personal testimony from TH)

Not all lectures go as planned. As an early career scholar I was asked to contribute to a one-day conference on the history of social welfare, and rather rashly decided that I would take the opportunity to engage with the work of an established scholar in my field, Joanna Innes.[8] And to do so by name.

It was a small conference and I saw the lecture as a chance to try out new ideas and approaches before a friendly audience. I also thought that I was approaching the issues about which Joanna Innes and I disagreed in a spirit of friendly debate. What I didn't expect was that Joanna would be sitting front and centre when I went up to the podium. I gave the paper as written, finding it hard not to notice Joanna's surprised expression. And when I had finished, she raised her hand and made the first intervention from the floor: 'I believe Tim Hitchcock and I disagree about many things, but do not believe he has identified a single one'. Joanna Innes then went on to dismantle my paper, point by point, leaving me entirely flummoxed, and drowning in public. I know that she recalls the occasion with great clarity, even thirty years later.

What I learned is that it is always better to build a positive case, based on clear evidence, than to try to tear down the work of others. Disagreements must be aired, but the historical content should be front and centre, rather than the historian. I also learned that you should never make assumptions about who is going to be sitting in the front row.

---

[8] Key publications of Joanna Innes, who was appointed to a post at Somerville College, Oxford, in 1982, include *Inferior Politics: Social Problems and Social Policies in Eighteenth-Century Britain* (Oxford, 2009); and, as editor with Mark Philp, *Re-Imagining Democracy in the Age of Revolutions: America, France, Britain, Ireland, 1750–1850* (Oxford, 2013).

14. Asking and answering seminar questions

SIGNPOST: Essential for researchers studying for higher degrees, and advice on participation in regular discussion groups is helpful for freelance researchers too.

Cheering the art of debate.

14.1 Regular seminar participation

Becoming a good researcher means much more than studying in isolation. An essential part of the learning process comes from regular participation at an academic seminar.[1] Even if the format seems initially strange (and most groups are welcoming these days and have open-house admission), it

---

[1] J. H. Anderson and A. H. Bellenkers, *Leading Dynamic Seminars: a Practical Handbook for University Educators* (Basingstoke, 2013).

is worth persevering. Seminars are access points to the world of sustained study. So all researchers should find an appropriate group and attend regularly. Many seminars form real communities, whose debates and ethos evolve over decades. Such groups are key antidotes to intellectual isolation. It's perennially instructive to learn about other projects and to assess how people use the chance to address a knowledgeable audience. By the same token, it's vital also to learn how to participate by studying the live arts of asking and answering questions.

Better still, it's highly educational not just to audit a seminar but also to participate actively. And that requirement entails being prepared regularly to ask probing questions; and being able, when giving one's own research presentation, to answer questions confidently and well.

The core reason for such participation is that a good seminar in effect provides a free consultancy for the speaker and an educational process for all present. Helping to create that positive experience boosts inner self-confidence; wins respect from supervisors and fellow researchers; and helps towards the advancement of knowledge and the making of communal judgements. It's an iterative process – and an excellent one in which to be not just a silent witness but an active participant.

These days, there's an increasing chance that the gathering will be organized virtually rather than face-to-face. All the advice here applies to all seminar formats. However, it's worth noting that speakers in virtual gatherings do not get the immediate feedback (ranging from laughter to murmured agreement or dissent) which 'real' participants spontaneously supply. So the first experience of talking to camera and being received in dead silence can prove somewhat disconcerting. The answer is to persevere, speaking succinctly – and making the voice and face as expressive as possible.

Researchers at all levels of experience are now learning this stylized version of speech. It constitutes a refinement of standard communication skills. The closest analogy is talking on the radio. Infusing the voice with warmth really helps – and, given the head-and-shoulders visibility of virtual conferencing, so does a warm smile.

14.2 The range of questions

Many straightforward enquiries exemplify a wholesome quest for further information or clarification. They ask for further detail about the sources, including their provenance and reliability. Or they seek further elaboration of the definitions and concepts that have been referenced. Sometimes, too, questioners will challenge a given terminology, even if still accepting the general thrust of an argument. Thus it often happens that requests for further information or clarification constitute the majority of all enquiries. It follows too that there is no presentation which cannot be questioned.[2] Every name, place, date or detail can prompt a follow-up request for further information.

By the way, it is wrong to assume that simple enquiries are somehow automatically 'inferior' or easier questions. One effective example was voiced after a presentation on the religious policy of the eighteenth-century British state and its dominions. The speaker had claimed that an inflexible Anglicanism was imposed everywhere. But one questioner asked simply: 'What about the Quebec Act?' Under this legislation (1774), Britain allowed freedom of worship to the French-speaking Quebec Catholics and enabled them to swear allegiance without reference to religion. This flexibility ran contrary to the speaker's stress upon the immovable Protestantism of British policy. Afterwards, it was generally agreed that the question was the verbal equivalent of a knock-out.

Another smaller but still substantial range of enquiries focuses upon the chosen methods of classification, selection and/or organization of research material. Challenges are especially required if the criteria have not been well explained in the presentation. Social-cultural classification systems, in particular, always benefit from debate, whether focusing upon class, ethnicity, religion, nationality or any other special identities. One phenomenon that is often under-studied is the extent of intermarriage between ostensibly different or even hostile groups. That process, which is very common historically, can greatly complicate assumptions about the rigidity of social divisions, and makes a good topic for questions. Most other systems of grouping data can be queried too. All such interventions can helpfully assist presenters to clarify what they have done and why.

Meanwhile, a minority of questions take the form of a direct conceptual challenge or philosophical counter-argument. Such strong interventions often provoke a lively general debate. One line of questioning is to consider the speaker's core argument and then assess whether it is internally consistent and upheld by the evidence. If not, then it's fairly open to challenge.

Another way of probing is to search for the speaker's underlying assumptions (maybe implicit rather than explicit) and then evaluate them. Perhaps the material could be used to make the opposite case – or at least to argue something very different. Such bracing questions are eminently valid. Sometimes those who raise fundamental objections don't necessarily endorse them but are playing devil's advocate. They are using the seminar

---

[2] L. Elder and R. Paul, *The Thinker's Guide to the Art of Asking Essential Questions* (Tomales, Calif., 2019); M. N. Browne and S. M. Keeley, *Asking the Right Questions: a Guide to Critical Thinking* (Boston, Mass., 2015).

as a forum for testing out ideas. At other times, questioners and presenter may discover that they disagree fundamentally. So be it, provided that the debates are conducted without aggression or personal animus.

If the speaker is a novice giving a first presentation, then the audience generally treats them comparatively gently (and the chair is usually protective too). By contrast, experienced figures will expect to get the compliment of a bracing set of questions, and will welcome a fundamental challenge. All should strive to be 'good seminar citizens': ready to enjoy the stimulus of debate.

Academic styles vary over time. At one stage, questions were asked aggressively, even savagely. But for the last thirty years or so, the prevalent style has become more courteous, even dulcet. However, the intellectual context of questions should not be diluted. In the seminar context, tough, well-honed, to-the-point criticisms are intellectually very helpful. As the poet-artist William Blake once remarked: 'Opposition is True Friendship'.[3] Good criticisms put speakers on their mettle. Sometimes, they are initially surprised; even indignant. But they should be triggered to defend and re-expound their arguments more effectively. That process also means that next time they present or write about this material they can anticipate and rebut criticisms in advance.

It's true that it takes a bit of debating experience to realize that a severe critic is in reality a friend lurking in disguise. But seminar participation is one of the best ways to learn.

14.3 Practising the art of questioning

Attracting the attention of the chair, indicating a willingness to ask something and then making a good intervention in a flowing debate is a creative skill and, like all skills, it is one that can be learned and improved with practice. Having taken the plunge, the process becomes steadily easier. By contrast, those who hesitate and remain silent find that it gets progressively more difficult to break into the debates. Hence all new researchers should be encouraged to start with short, punchy, wholesome requests for information.

Any intervention that launches one's voice into the room is good. In that way, new questioners can get used to the rustle of accompanying attention, which can at first seem off-putting. Then, over time, researchers can progress to making longer enquiries and eventually to offering counter-arguments.

---

[3] Illustration in William Blake's *Marriage of Heaven and Hell* (London, 1793), showing a writhing serpent of knowledge and the faded words: 'Opposition is True Friendship'.

Such attempted refutations, by the way, should be kept relatively brief. It's very bad form to launch into a lengthy counter-lecture. Any questioners who detect signs of that tendency in themselves should control it quickly. Otherwise they are likely to become classic audience bores, causing others to sigh heavily and rustle papers to deter them. The focus should remain throughout upon the presenter and the content of the presentation.

Some supervisors these days require research students to ask a given number of questions per academic year (rising in number as the years pass). That instruction sounds a bit mechanical. But it provides excellent training because, actually, it is easier to ask a question when the decision to intervene has already been made. Otherwise, a lot of time is spent dithering: *shall I, shan't I?* Afterwards, it's also good practice for postgraduates to review their intervention with the supervisor. Generally, newcomers to the art are buoyed by a successful first question – breaking their seminar duck – and gain confidence for next time.

If there is great competition to join the debates, as sometimes happens, then not everyone will manage to speak every time. Nonetheless, it's excellent mental practice for all auditors to cudgel their brains throughout the presentation, whether they succeed in joining the debate or not. The minimum target is to devise at least one potential question. It's a great way to remain intellectually alert. And, having become accustomed to that good practice, more advanced targets can be set. It's a subtle task to devise three different questions: one in the form of a general enquiry to start the questioning; the second a definitional question to probe more deeply; and the third a seriously tough critique, in case the meeting is giving an experienced speaker too easy a ride.

Such mental preparation is also helpful for those who are invited to chair seminars and lectures (see chapter 15). It has the further advantage in that if summoned unexpectedly to ask a question (rare, but it does happen), then something apposite is ready to hand. With these matters to occupy the listening mind, no seminar presentation is ever boring.

14.4 *The need for effective answers*

Both the audience's questions and the speaker's answers are crucial. In general, their specific wording remains non-memorable. But, while the details of questions and answers are subsumed into the broad academic debate, the nature of the answers matters just as much as does the thrust of the questions. Effective responses greatly enhance a good presentation. By contrast, poor and/or evasive answers can backfire. Indeed, at worst, they can ruin a superficially fine presentation by failing to rebut a fundamental criticism.

Hence the overwhelming rule is to reply rather than to sidestep the question. Nothing is more annoying for an academic audience than to realize that the presenter is intellectually absconding. (In politics, the art of evasion has become so highly developed that even the toughest and most persistent interviewer may find it impossible to extract an answer.[4] But academic life has a different set of expectations.)

One possible diversionary tactic is to attack the motives and probity of the questioner. Yet responses of that sort cut absolutely no ice in an academic seminar. Audiences think poorly of all speakers who evade questions and refuse to enter into debate. A general seminar convention, which is almost invariably upheld, requires both engagement and complete courtesy. On the rare occasions when someone (whether the speaker or a member of the audience) is personally abusive or unduly aggressive, then the entire room turns against the person who is being rude (or rudest). The chair may also intervene, depending on the circumstances, to halt unpleasant exchanges. In sporting terms, the correct advice is to kick the ball, not the player. As already indicated, however, hostile comments are very unusual during academic meetings.

Very terse replies are also unhelpful ways of evading discussion. Single-word answers, such as 'Yes' or 'No', generate an initial laugh, especially when following an over-long and tedious question. Yet such extreme brevity is not really playing fair with either the questioner or the audience. It *is* fine, meanwhile, to start an answer with a single brisk word, provided that the respondent then goes on to justify the verdict. Then the speaker gets approval for providing both clarity and content.

Overall, there's a balance to be struck. Answers to questions should be not too short but ... not too lengthy either. If anything, respondents tend to speak for slightly too long, often in their anxiety to cover every nuance. These days, however, chairs usually try to keep a good flow of questions coming. If and when speakers are unwisely tempted to give a reprise of their entire presentations, the audience quickly switches off. The same applies when evasive answers turn into nothing more than higher waffle. A crisp response, answering the point(s) – and nothing more – works best. Also, crispness allows time for more questions, to the benefit of both speakers and audiences. As a broad generalization, the seminar time is expected to be divided approximately fifty/fifty between the presentation and the discussion – with forty-five to fifty minutes given to each half – although in some national traditions – disappointingly – very little, if any, time is allotted for questions.

---

[4] J. Baggini, *Do They Think You're Stupid? 100 Ways of Spotting Spin and Nonsense from the Media, Pundits and Politicians* (London, 2010).

14.5 Tips for answering

A first pointer for respondents is to start with a short 'holding' phrase, which provides a brief moment for cogitation. When listening to a complex or tricky question, it can be difficult to grasp the real point *and* simultaneously formulate a good answer. But many respondents find that while starting with something pleasant, like 'I'm glad that you raised that point', their subconscious minds are getting into gear. In other words, speakers have given themselves a short mental breathing space. However, it's sensible to use many variants of such 'holding' phrases. It sounds too saccharine if every question is welcomed with the same apparent rapture in identical phraseology.

While listening to a question, it's very helpful for speakers to have discreetly at hand a notepad on which they can jot down very short headings that indicate the topic(s) raised. Having that reminder is especially useful in the event of two-pronged questions. When answering one half of a query, it's too easy to forget about the other half. Looking down to check one's notes can provide a useful prompt. Furthermore, a brief memorandum of the points raised by the audience is an invaluable recourse. Their comments and queries may be intricate or plain-sailing. But, either way, they tell speakers which elements of their analyses need clarification and where the arguments need bolstering.

Hence it is good practice to institute an auto-debriefing fairly soon after every public presentation (before the debate has faded from the mind). The notes can be expanded into a mini-review, to keep on file for one's own eyes only. Then, should speakers wish to revisit the material (for example, when writing research chapters), they have an instant critique to hand. Next time, they can either improve their work and refute criticisms more successfully; or instead, they can accept the criticisms and switch their core argument. Such complete reversals happen relatively rarely. Yet the point of exploring ideas in open debate is to offer options for intellectual growth, which may lead in unexpected directions.

It follows also that, in the interests of frankness, speakers should never pretend to knowledge they don't have. If unable to formulate an answer immediately, which is a problem that can happen to anyone on a bad day (or when presenting new and untested material at the research frontier), the best reply is: 'That's a great question. I don't know the answer off-hand; but I will check it out and get back to you'. And, having promised, then it's naturally important for speakers to deliver. Audiences will cheerfully accept a frank confession of an inability to answer immediately. They greatly prefer that to listening to prevarication and fudge-and-mudge. Following up a question in this way also provides an opportunity for longer correspondence and engagement.

Above all, the key point for respondents is to stand fast on their core arguments. It is acceptable to give way graciously when faced with minor challenges, if they are well posed. Accepting valid corrections is part of the give-and-take of the debating process. On central elements of the argument, however, speakers are expected to stand their ground, politely but firmly. Later on, people can reconsider and change their minds – which does happen, albeit rarely. But after a presentation that has attracted probing questions, the audience expects the core case to be defended in full.

An excellent example occurred at a meeting of the American Historical Association in December 1996. The eminent social historian Lawrence Stone was in a crowded conference session where his latest publication was given a searching critique by a new researcher.[5] Standing up, he exclaimed: 'Oh, dear, I think I've been holed below the water-line'. Then, with a cheerful laugh (shared with the audience), Stone rallied and, on the spur of the moment, articulated a robust response to the (valid) criticism. He was neither rancorous nor flustered. It was a sparkling moment, showcasing academic debate at its best. Stone was arguing for the exclusivity of aristocratic lifestyles in the later seventeenth century. By contrast, his critic found the personnel of commercial, professional and landed society to be overlapping.

Adding to the interest of the occasion was the fact that Stone's critic was one of his own postgraduate students. But he was utterly fair-minded. He fully supported Susan Whyman, the postgraduate in question, who is now a distinguished freelance historian.[6] Thus, while some established professors cultivate in-groups of close supporters, the more generous ones, like Stone, are dedicated to the advancement of historical knowledge, even when their own arguments come under attack.

14.6 Summary: not always one right question or answer but a right process of debate

Manifestly, there can be no one right answer in absolutely all cases. Some historical issues are too intractable, and some sources are too fragmentary, to be resolved into one single unanimously agreed outcome.

---

[5] The rival views eventually appeared in print. Compare L. Stone and J. C. F. Stone, *An Open Elite? England, 1540–1880* (London, 1984); and S. E. Whyman, 'Land and trade revisited: the case of John Verney, London merchant and baronet, 1660–1720', *London Journal*, xxii (1997), 16–32.

[6] S. E. Whyman, *The Pen and the People: English Letters Writers, 1660–1800* (Oxford, 2009); *The Useful Knowledge of William Hutton: Culture and Industry in Eighteenth-Century Birmingham* (Oxford, 2018).

There is, however, a right process of firm and thorough but courteous debate.[7] That's the aim of a seminar and often the outcome. Speakers should be ready to respond appropriately. Replies should be brief, pertinent and positive. It's good to learn from the questions and the responses. It's nice to win the argument as well. Above all, therefore, all parties should remain on their toes intellectually. Having given a presentation, it's fatal to relax too soon. Equally, it's fatal to underestimate an audience. Anyone, whether highly trained or a complete novice, can ask a searching question. There's always scope for an unexpected angle or a fresh critique.

Questioners and respondents are sustaining an impromptu debate, until the chair finally winds up proceedings, usually with thanks all round. The collective sense of the historian's discipline is forged in many arenas; but the interactive format of the seminars, combined with the regularity of their meetings, makes them particularly crucial. Even if specific presentations seem boring, the deeper overall processes are not. Participants may try to move the debates onwards by (politely worded) probing questions, conceptual challenges and deep theoretical disagreements, excluding only personal rudeness, slander and hate speech. And, out of reasoned argument comes knowledge.

[7] J. Brimble and D. Pritchard, *Guide to Debating: the Principles and Practice of Debate* (Pontypridd, 2003); R. Feldman, *Reason and Argument* (Harlow, 2014); D. Walton, *Argument Evaluation and Evidence* (Cham, 2016).

15. Chairing seminars and lectures

SIGNPOST: Relevant to all researchers

Praising the art of sympathetic chairing.

15.1 The art of chairing

The aim is to get everyone involved in a really effective discussion, aiding the speaker and all participants at public lectures or academic seminars. 'Effective' in this context means a debate that is both critical and supportive. Any criticisms, of course, should be directed at the contents of the lecture or seminar paper, not the speaker. As has been already noted, players should sportingly kick the ball, not the opponent. Or the same point can be made another way, for those who don't like or understand sporting metaphors. Viewpoints and ideas can be robustly challenged without demeaning fellow debaters. An idea is not shown to be right or wrong simply by reference to the person who expresses it. The arguments, not the argumentative individuals, are under scrutiny. And the chair, like a sporting referee or umpire, should facilitate fair play.

Fine: all that sounds tolerably easy. In fact, however, chairing is a considerable art that can, furthermore, be learned.[1] One good method when attending seminars and lectures is to analyse the various chairing styles. Which work? Which don't? Does the chair keep things running to time? Play fair by all parties, protecting both the speaker and the questioners from over-the-top accusations? The ideal is to facilitate stimulating debates which involve and energize everyone in attendance. Watching and learning from chairing styles is a good way of keeping amused and interested throughout a lecture or seminar, whether the event is a success or otherwise.

At the same time, the acoustics and room layout, sometimes known as 'room dynamics', can either ease or complicate the chair's task.[2] For a formal lecture it's okay to have people seated in straight lines; but for an academic seminar, it's best to place chairs around a table, or, if that is not possible, then at least to arrange the seating into semi-circles, focusing upon the central speaker, rather than rigid lines. These details have a subliminal effect. So it's helpful if the chair can check the venue in advance – even five minutes in advance, if no more – to ensure an environment conducive to collective debate.

15.2 Opening the proceedings

Opening the proceedings calls for an open and genial manner, with a joke, or failing that, at least a humorous tone. Then the speaker can be introduced pithily, without notes. There's no need for a lengthy recitation of everything that he or she has ever done. That tactic just makes audiences bored and drowsy. And it's seriously unhelpful to announce in advance the key points that the speaker will be making. That manoeuvre falls doubly flat. It annoys and disconcerts the speaker, while it makes audiences bored and restive, wondering why they have to sit through something that they have already been told.

Instead, the chair's task is to bond the meeting together. A constructive but unobtrusive way of doing that is to look, visibly and fairly slowly, all

[1] See C. O'Connor, *The View from the Chair: the Art of Chairing Meetings* (Ballivor, Co. Meath, 1994), and many websites with online advice. The classic handbook on the 20th-century Labour movement was W. Citrine's *ABC of Chairmanship* (London, 1939; frequently reprinted, most recently by the Fabian Society in 2016).

[2] D. Kantor, *Reading the Room: Group Dynamics for Coaches and Leaders* (San Francisco, Calif., 2012).

around the room. As already noted, a 'lighthouse beam' brings everyone together within an encompassing gaze. (See section 13.3 for the same advice to speakers.) It's disastrous to stare intently at individuals. But a light rotating gaze indicates that the chair's attention is directed to all quarters of the room. Throughout the presentation, whether good, bad or indifferent, the chair's task is also to look alert and interested. Such an attitude encourages everyone. And it's helpful to follow things closely, since upon occasions the speaker will suddenly appeal to the chair (perhaps to ask how much time is left). Actually, the need to concentrate is one good reason for agreeing to chair. It keeps one wide awake.

Ideally, speakers should have been briefed beforehand about the length of talk required. However, the chair should always confirm/reconfirm that information at the start, and then gently halt speakers who go on for too long. On a formal platform, it may be necessary to pass a pre-printed card saying *TIME!* to the speaker. But if people are sitting close together and able to detect body language, then an informal hand signal and a meaningful look will usually suffice. There's always some leeway, but if the speaker is part of a panel then strict time-keeping is essential to be fair to all contributors. In other circumstances, however, it's the chair's judgement call.

15.3 *Chairing the questions*

While the speaker is talking, it's helpful for the chair to make a mental (or scribbled) list of a number of key questions raised by the presentation. An attentive seminar or lecture audience will usually spot all or most of the points for discussion. But shrewd anticipation makes the chair's task easier. Immediately after the presentation has ended, it's essential to make some suitable preliminary response while people gather their thoughts. It's always bad news when the chair just says abruptly: 'Any questions?' And even worse when there's a great silence and the chair adds dolefully: 'Well, I can see it's going to be a difficult session'. Lead balloons all round.

Instead, the chair should briefly thank the speaker (nothing over the top) and note some issues raised by the paper (that's helpful for non-experts in the audience). Then it's best for the chair to ask an opening question, to get the discussion going. It should not be too heavy, but not a patsy either. As the speaker starts to answer, the chair then looks intently round the room, seeking signals from people who wish to ask a question. This technique is the really crucial bit. If at all possible, the chair should sit up, or semi-stand, leaning against a chair or table, to free the sightlines. Then the lighthouse beam can skim lightly round the room. Preferably with a smile. People usually give imperceptible signals – a nod or lift of the hand, rather like the sly nods and winks from buyers at an auction. Chairs therefore have to be very vigilant. They are trying to foster a sense of community – and newcomers in particular can feel distinctly rebuffed if their overly cautious signs go unnoticed. If in doubt, therefore, chairs should not hesitate to ask individuals if a passing gesture was actually a request to speak.

Usually, the questions are taken in the order that they come. It's not unusual for the first moments of a discussion to be rather quiet. But momentum soon develops as the shape of the debate begins to emerge. The chair always has some leeway. If there's a long list of keen people, it can be helpful to change the sequence to ensure that questions come from all different parts of the room. That practice draws everyone into the discussion. But it's important not to leave anyone out. Overlooking would-be questioners generates bad feelings and accusations of bias. Allowing experienced figures to dominate the discussion is equally unhelpful. If time is running seriously short, the chair should advise the room of that fact, and urge the remaining questioners to be very brief.

Sometimes, either the questions or the speaker's answers become too lengthy and risk turning into an alternative lecture. In those circumstances, the audience will be grateful for the chair to intervene. Often a hand signal can be used to break the flow, followed by a gentle reminder that time is running short. As already noted, it's rare (in academic life) that questions are formulated or asked rudely. If it should happen, however, the chair should intervene, extracting the element within the question that can be answered and telling the speaker to ignore the rest. Or, if the question is completely out of order, the chair should simply say so.

Even more rarely, one or more individuals in the audience can go into a rant about some topical or emotional issue of the day. It's again the task of the chair to intervene politely but firmly to halt the disruption. Often, the mood of the meeting will additionally make itself clear – usually on the side of the chair and against interruption. In the most extreme cases – which are very rare in the academic world – the chair should ask the disrupters to leave; and if order cannot be restored, then the chair should close the meeting, with apologies and a promise to reconvene. Such scenarios are highly unusual, but they do occur from time to time, usually when contentious topics are being discussed by contentious speakers. Hence it's always worth being prepared.

More mundane difficulties can also occur if questions are poorly phrased or incomprehensible. The speaker is entitled to look to the chair for help. In such circumstances, the question should be paraphrased into something answerable. Very rarely, there are interventions which remain impenetrable.

In such cases, either the chair or the speaker may invite the questioner to make the point in full afterwards, either in person or in writing.

Discreetly, then, the chair is conducting the debate, and should have a range of issues to raise if the questioning flags. Difficult questions (see section 14.2) can be used especially against the good and the great, who shouldn't be let off too easily. First-timers, however, should not be given too hard a time – enough to test them, but not to destroy their confidence. If they are seriously floundering, then some supportive words from the chair will be appropriate. The seminar is intended as a high-powered exchange of views, not a blood-sport.

15.4 Sustaining camaraderie

These days, the preferred style of a public lecture or seminar is one of academic camaraderie. And most groups are delighted to engage accordingly. In the very old days, it was often the practice for questions to be asked by the academics in order of seniority of appointment. The most venerable professor would open the proceedings and the rest duly await their turn. But such hierarchic formality has generally disappeared, though there are still variations in questioning styles between different academic cultures, according to long-standing traditions.

Setting a more contemporary tone is the task of the chair, who should try to strike a genial balance. The aim is to be friendly, but not overly fulsome. A gushing style just sounds sycophantic. At the same time, the chair must be critical but not *too* sardonic. He or she should not try to steal the limelight, which properly belongs to the speaker. So the chair may try to be smart but should not become too sharp or polemical.

All members of the participating audience – and their questions – should be equally welcomed. It's best to avoid calling people to speak by their academic titles and/or names or, even worse, by familiar nicknames. Such in-references make any group seem far too cliquey. Newcomers feel alienated, as they subliminally receive the message that only those known to the chair are really welcome. Calling questioners to speak can therefore be done by a mixture of looks, gestures and reference to room location: 'Now a question from the back', and so forth. (These conventions, however, are being updated for the world of video-conferencing. In that case, questions can be submitted in writing, allowing the chair to group and call them thematically.)

Having been given the floor, it's customary for questioners to give their names briefly. Most do so, although some mumble pretty unintelligibly. But it's not worth the chair intervening to insist on absolute clarity, since that halts the flow. It's good practice in regular seminars, by the way, to invite all participants to identify themselves at the start of each academic cycle. In one-off meetings, that procedure is not always practical. Yet the principle remains clear in all circumstances that questioners should be ready to share their identities as part of a shared intellectual community.

Developing a sense of camaraderie is a process to which all seminar participants contribute. Only very rarely do audiences remain unhappy or restive. But in all cases it falls to the chair to give a significant lead, by fostering an atmosphere of friendly inclusivity. It's particularly important to welcome occasional attendees as well as regulars. There is often a considerable turnover of people from one session to the next. Unless newcomers are made welcome, attendances will fall, draining the events of intellectual renewal and energy. One pleasant way to include everyone is to organize some informal sociability either before or after these academic sessions. And if that is done, it's helpful for the chair, as host, to ensure unobtrusively that no-one is left standing miserably on the margins, without talking to anyone. Getting people to chat together in informal sessions helps to prepare the ground for high-powered but courteous discussion in the formal sessions. Indeed, as already noted, the best antidote to any potential feelings of intellectual isolation is research camaraderie.

15.5 Summary: an art that conceals art

After a lecture or seminar, it's the paper or lecture that rightly gets remembered – and then, perhaps, the discussion. Big, complex issues are anyway not resolved easily. They often take many debates; plus more research; and then more debates.

Yet the art of constructive chairing makes a major contribution to scholarship, which relies upon reasoned debate. As researchers hope for their own presentations to be intelligently discussed, so when chairing they should do for others what they would like done for themselves.

Orchestrating a research debate is a task done in plain sight, but unobtrusively. At its best, therefore, it is an art that conceals art to produce gold-dust.

15.6 Coda: a historic example of great chairing in response to an unexpected heckle (personal testimony from PJC)

Once, unintentionally, I heckled the speakers at an academic conference. It was in the early 1970s, and my spontaneous outcry generated such a great response from the chair that it deserves to go onto the historical record. Two hundred or more academics were crowded within the University of London's large Beveridge Hall, where two eminent historians, the established figure of Hugh Trevor-Roper[3] and the younger up-and-coming Keith Thomas,[4] had been invited for a special public debate. They had already jousted fiercely in print about seventeenth-century witchcraft, and this event was organized by the History Board of Studies of University of London so that the arguments could continue in public. It was a mark of how seriously the debates were being taken – and the packed hall paid testimony to the great scholarly interest. Yet face-to-face, as often happens among academics (not so much among politicians), the antagonists were very polite to each other and didn't really engage with their differences. The occasion as a whole proved to be a damp squib.

There was, however, one moment of excitement. One of the speakers referred rather contemptuously to the characteristic victims of witchcraft accusations as 'useless old women'. Without having intended to do so, I immediately cried out, firmly and clearly, 'Shame!' Everyone sitting around me recoiled. The speakers said nothing. After a moment of deep silence, however, the meeting's chair, the historian Joel Hurstfield,[5] responded with immense aplomb, by saying: '*Madam, contain your just indignation!*'

Brilliant! His old-fashioned courtesy effectively rebuked my uncouthness. Yet he upheld my complaint, accepting that the tone of the debate had been too dismissive of the women accused of witchcraft. Immediately, the people sitting around me smiled with relief and reversed their physical recoil. This intervention on my part produced a short flare of excitement, after which the fairly halting discussion was resumed. It is unlikely that anyone else recalls either the event or this exchange. Nonetheless, this tactic of affirmation-plus-rebuke should rank very high on the list of effective ways of coping with hecklers. A tip for chairs to remember, should meetings ever get rowdy.[6]

---

[3] H. R. Trevor-Roper, historian and polemicist, was author of, *inter alia*, *Archbishop Laud, 1573–1645* (London, 1940); *The Last Days of Hitler* (London, 1947); *The European Witch-Craze of the Sixteenth and Seventeenth Centuries and Other Essays* (London, 1969); and *The Invention of Scotland: Myth and History*, ed. J. J. Carter (London, 2008). For critical appreciations, see A. Sisman, *Hugh Trevor-Roper: the Biography* (London, 2010); B. Worden (ed.), *Hugh Trevor-Roper: the Historian* (London, 2016).

[4] For his social-anthropological approach, sustained throughout his oeuvre, see K. Thomas, *Religion and the Decline of Magic*; *Man and the Natural World*; *The Ends of Life*; and *In Pursuit of Civility*.

[5] The Tudor specialist J. Hurstfield wrote on 16th-century England, including notably *Freedom, Corruption and Government in Elizabethan England* (London, 1973).

[6] In case of need, see also K. Fields, *How to Handle Hecklers: the Complete Guide to Handling Every Performer's Worst Nightmare* (London, 2006, 2013): <https://www.howto handlehecklers.com> [accessed 30 April 2021].

16. Taking the last steps to completion

SIGNPOST: Particularly relevant to researchers studying for higher degrees, but general advice on finishing a large written project is relevant to all.

Recognizing that completion always takes longer than expected, and sticking at the task.

16.1 The importance of the long, last steps

The first big rule is that finishing a big research project always takes longer than expected. Completion is inspiring, energizing ... but simultaneously painstaking and nit-picking. Which means (to repeat) that it takes longer than expected. And, then again, longer than that.

There's no doubt that the finishing stages can be very frustrating, both for researchers and for friends and family, who are often awaiting completion impatiently. Authors can particularly confuse themselves if they work on several different draft versions at the same time. The golden rule is always to mark obsolete texts as such (filing them separately), so that attention is focused upon the one top copy. Then it's necessary to work steadily through the completion stages, since the quality of the exposition always improves during the last iterations.[1] Each run-through reveals the general argument more clearly. Rather as a sculptor sees, with each chip from the chisel, the finished statue emerging from the block of marble, so the historical researcher sees, with each concluding polish, the whole picture fall into shape.

Work for a doctoral thesis, which has to be of publishable standard, has to be as near perfect in content and presentation as possible. (In that regard, submitting advanced research is qualitatively different from submitting BA essays or MA dissertations, where different regulations apply.) Getting research work into its final form thus means checking every detail, down to every last footnote, plus every last dot and comma. *What?* apprentice researchers sometimes scream, incredulously: *Every dot and comma? You must be joking.*

Yet it's no joke. Research work that is not properly presented is sent back unread by publishers and journal editors. And in the case of a doctoral thesis, the examination is a supreme test of presentation as well as of content. Thus, if there are some missing dots and commas, the examiners will furnish a list of points for correction before the thesis can be accepted.

Indeed, if presentation of the text of a would-be doctoral thesis is a complete mess, the examiners can ask for the entire document to be revised – rather than having themselves to list thousands of small errors. They are not proofreaders. So it's vital always to check and then to check again, with the closest attention. Presenting research material to a high standard should have been inculcated from the very start of the doctoral programme. Yet any researchers who find that this aspect of their training has been neglected should not hesitate, even close to the end, to ask for suitable advice on improvements. It's a learning curve up until the very last moment. Happily, these days it has become immeasurably easier to get the presentation right. Grammar- and spell-checkers provide technical proofreaders. Computer-generated notes and bibliography (see chapter 6) also allow materials to be compiled thoroughly and accurately. As a result, the technical quality of theses presented today is usually very good to excellent, to the joy of examiners.

---

[1] K. Guccione and J. Wellington, *Taking Control of Writing Your Thesis: a Guide to Get You to the End* (London, 2017); H. Kara, *Finishing Your PhD: What You Need to Know* (Kindle edn, 2016), for which see <https://helenkara.com/2016/09/14/finishing-your-phd-what-you-need-to-know> [accessed 30 April 2021].

16.2 Perfecting layout and presentation

Just as historical research combines practical and conceptual skills, so the presentation of research has to meet both practical and conceptual targets. Readers must not be distracted from the analytical flow by sloppy or inadequate layout, or by faulty referencing. Hence all text and supporting tables, figures, notes and any other documentation must be clear, accessible and pleasant to the reader's eye. Specifically, too, all instructions from the relevant university examination board must be followed scrupulously. Each institution has its own set of requirements, which are clearly available, usually on a department or university website. Often, instructions are formulated according to standard publishing conventions, used globally, and it is also worth consulting standard reference works such as Butcher's *Copy-editing*.[2] Yet there are sufficient variations between systems to make it imperative to check in close detail.

Headings and sub-headings should be in standardized format. Tables, illustrations, graphs, maps and all other visual materials should be clearly presented and labelled.

'Widows and orphans' should be avoided. That arresting phrase is the old proofreader's term calling for corrections to page layout. 'Orphans' refers to the lonely appearance of a single line of text starting a new paragraph at the foot of a page, without subsequent lines in support. 'Widows', by contrast, refers to the dejected appearance of only a few words which may be marooned at the top of an otherwise blank page or column – say, at the end of a chapter. Reader-friendly page layout thus seeks to remove all jarring visual effects.

Modern word processors normally prevent 'widows and orphans' automatically, but won't catch all infelicities. The location of tables and images can be particularly awkward. Making minor changes to correct the layout is an acknowledgement of concern for the eventual readership. It's a task that needs to be completed at the very end, just before final submission of the typescript. Otherwise, the process of revising may accidentally produce a page layout that just doesn't look right, and which can make the argument difficult to follow.

Spelling, punctuation and layout must also be checked systematically throughout, in accordance with the specified conventions. That task has been set not only to show respect for readers, but also to indicate that the researcher can successfully meet a professional requirement. The same

---

[2] Classic guidance is provided by J. Butcher, C. Drake and M. Leach (ed.), *Butcher's Copy-Editing: the Cambridge Handbook for Editors, Copy-Editors and Proofreaders* (Cambridge, 2006), and there are many web guides to professional presentation.

point applies to the provision of thorough documentation in the form of notes (whether footnotes or endnotes). No joy is generated when and if authors invent their own system of annotation. Instead, the usual response is irritation.

Sometimes scholars have to grit their teeth when asked to follow conventions which they dislike personally. But readers need homogeneous texts, so that they can concentrate on the contents, and not get distracted by glitches or inconsistencies. Authors therefore have to bite the bullet and follow accurately whatever presentational conventions they have been asked to adopt.

As already stressed, the final formatting and polishing can take much more time than anticipated. It often takes multiple run-throughs of the chapters, separately finalizing the text, and then checking the format, layout and notes. Therefore researchers should never rush to tell the world that the task is done before it is absolutely done. Or, even worse, deceive themselves! Clear-eyed realism is useful at all times – and absolutely imperative when completing a major project, based on years of slog. By the way, it can be tedious, to put it mildly, to reread the umpteenth draft of one's own work; and errors can slip past through sheer familiarity. Hence the advantage of getting the text read by supervisors and (if available) by critical friends with an eye for copy-editing.

16.3 Pulling the threads together

During the pulling of many threads into one big picture, it's not usually necessary to remodel the entire text. A researcher's general style and approach becomes apparent in the course of writing. And the constant review process means that the length, sequence and thrust of the different chapters should have been continually adjusted during the course of production.

Nonetheless, during the last iterations, there are some useful exercises that can be undertaken to pull the threads together clearly. It's particularly helpful to review and adjust the full list of chapter titles and sub-titles, when appropriate. These need to be presented in a compatible style. They should signal an unfolding argument. As a general rule, too, they should not be too wordy, unless wordiness has been specially chosen for some particular purpose. In sum, the chapter titles should be neither too abstruse nor too simplistic. The aim is to attract readers and to signal them through the journey.

After that, it's equally important to check the sequence of the research chapters. The early sections dealing with definitions and source surveys must retain their position at the start. Yet the thematic chapters may be subject to variation. Historical analyses do not automatically have to be presented as chronological narratives. They can appear as different thematic strands of an overall picture. Of course, the scope for changes won't be infinite. Yet it may be that a late shuffling of the chapters, thinking about how to sustain interest, will improve matters. It's also worth reflecting that sometimes material needs to be condensed or sections removed entirely. More is not always better.

Having reviewed both chapter titles and chapter sequence, it's then helpful to undertake a very quick and targeted rewriting. A sequential check through the text should be done as impartially as possible. If there are beautiful sections which don't really belong in the current study, then they should be axed and kept for later. Yet there may also be three or four key places in the study, which become apparent only at the end, where an important point should be highlighted or inserted, with a cross-reference to the general theme. Those iterated and reiterated punch-points help to knit the whole thing together.

It's also good to check the final sentence of each chapter: is it clear and summative? And does the first sentence of the following chapter lead on positively, but without boring repetition? This particular exercise in checking/rewriting should be done relatively quickly and easily, right at the end. It emphatically does not call for new research at such a late stage. It's a matter of checking for what film-makers call 'continuity'.

In some old films, the checkers slept on the job, and characters in one frame wear clothing which doesn't match with their garb in the next. Such vagaries can be endearing. One celebrated example is Cary Grant's inconsistent neck-tie in his first long scene with Rosalind Russell in *His Girl Friday* (1940), a screwball comedy directed by Howard Hawks. The two stars joust verbally, as they represent a newspaper editor and his former ace-reporter who is also his ex-wife. Cleverly, the director has spliced the different takes together to produce a witty, supremely quick-fire dialogue. But the 'continuity' experts failed to note that Grant's tie hangs in a different alignment from frame to frame. Perhaps its wonkiness is subliminally showing the editor's agitation on re-encountering his ex-wife, who is about to marry someone else. Or perhaps the director prized the power of the dialogue over the visual impact. Either way, the blunder has become a known eccentricity in the annals of film.

By contrast, a research thesis does not get such indulgence. The calling-card of a doctorate is its precision and accuracy. Linkage exercises for clear continuity therefore add a fine corroborative polish to an unfolding argument.

16.4 Incorporating a self-reflexive statement

Crucial also in the very final stages is the exercise of self-reflexivity, which asks researchers to incorporate a short personal statement of their broad approach. The aim is not to write a full intellectual autobiography, although some historians later do so very interestingly.[3] Instead, the intention is to frame the study by providing some key information about the researcher. These days, too, many institutions of higher education ask prospective students to supply 'reflexive statements' as part of their applications,[4] as do numerous employers. Hence, for researchers, this exercise is a specific application of what is becoming a widespread practice of expressive self-awareness.[5]

Considered reflections often start by explaining how and why the research topic was chosen. They then note the broad approach, plus any special attitudes to gender, ethnicity, class, religion, politics or other big issues (as relevant), which might affect the overall analysis. This exercise in intellectual self-presentation is best done with a judicious combination of truth with tact. It's not a moment for jocular self-deprecation, such as confessing oneself to be 'an idle layabout' or a 'confused borrower of ideas from others'.

On the contrary, the self-reflexive statement should be probing and earnest, explaining the researcher's intellectual journey. And, while generally written near the end of the project, it usually appears within chapter 1. Just to repeat: it's best to avoid being too bland (unhelpful) or too chatty (annoying). Personal authenticity is what's needed, in the spirit of the project that is nearing completion. (In all circumstances, it's imperative to avoid online services offering phoney personal statements for sale. Fake identities and false credentials seriously corrode social trust.)[6] Hence the best motto is the Shakespearian: 'To thine own self be true …', with literary tact and intellectual honesty.

16.5 Honing the conclusion

Writing the conclusion to a big research study is a particularly powerful moment. It often happens that the full import of the overall argument

[3] For this genre, see Popkin, *History, Historians and Autobiography*; and R. J. D. Munro, *Clio's Lives: Biographies and Autobiographies of Historians* (Canberra, 2017).

[4] In the UK, the Universities and Colleges Admissions Service (UCAS) provides a useful guide: <https://www.ucas.com/undergraduate/applying-university/how-write-ucas-undergraduate-personal-statement> [accessed 30 April 2021].

[5] A. Baron, 'Get that job: personal statements', <https://methods.sagepub.com/video/get-that-job-personal-statements> [accessed 9 Feb. 2022].

[6] See A. Attrill, *The Manipulation of Online Presentation: Create, Edit, Re-Edit and Present* (Basingstoke, 2015); C. Rosenthal and S. Schäfer (ed.), *Fake Identity? The Impostor Narrative in North American Culture* (Frankfurt, 2014).

becomes apparent only at the very end, when all the material is brought together. Researchers should thus set aside some quiet time in order to read steadily through all the chapters, in their now final sequence.

This exercise is not a moment for brainstorming and deciding to do something completely different. Instead, it's time for the closest of focus, thinking hard about the arguments and how best to conclude them. At this stage, it's usual to find that very frequent consultations with supervisors are needed, for their experienced input.

It should therefore be no surprise to find that writing the final chapter often necessitates some adaptations or changed emphases to earlier chapters. That's part of the editing process. In particular, it's very common to find that, having written the last chapter, the introduction needs to be rewritten or adjusted as well. The research process constitutes an intellectual journey – and the first chapter may have pointed towards a destination which was not eventually the one that was reached. Such final changes are good signs that the research has achieved something new and initially unexpected.

While revising the final chapter, it's useful to cross-check with any provisional big points that have been identified at earlier stages of the project – and jotted down in an interim research diary, if one has been kept (see section 3.4). In that way, researchers are reminded of their own accumulating thoughts. And the final advice to adjust or recheck the first chapter, which can seem like a drastic shaking of the foundations (*rewrite chapter 1?!*), can be implemented relatively rapidly and simply. Indeed, it can prove a pleasant, even cheerful process, as the initial stage-setting is aligned with all that follows.

So crucial is the final iteration that, while the early chapters should always be written to a high standard, they should not be considered as completed until the whole thesis is edited as one.

Through years of intensive work on a big project, individual researchers have genuinely become world experts on their subjects. The final summation records their working synthesis, on which they are willing to rest their case. (It's not necessary to solve the mysteries of the entire universe. It's enough to own one original foothold.) The final message should be crystallized into a magisterial last sentence. It can be short and snappy or gracious and balanced, as seems best. But not verbose, orotund and diffuse. And the final message must, of course, relate to the study's overall findings.

There's no point in giving a final flourish that flies off the point. A proportion of readers actually start by checking a book's conclusion; and some read no more. If all they then recall is off the point, then the exercise has misfired. Conclusions should be definitively on message – and expressed with full conviction!

16.6 Summary: the final full stop

Completing a first big history project is a huge milestone for any researcher. It is therefore one to be savoured. Immediately, doctoral supervisors will be organizing the appointment of examiners, and advising on preparations for the viva (see chapter 17). Researchers, at the same time, may feel a tangle of emotions. Relief and happiness can battle with sadness at the end of a fascinating and absorbing journey.

Sometimes, researchers at the very last may be reluctant to let go, even if they have been dreaming of completion for months. These conflicting emotions are very human. Thus, while there is a syndrome known as fear-of-never-finishing, there is also a rival fear-of-actually-finishing.

Supervisors, with the help of colleagues in each department or faculty – and fellow students – should manage to diminish such apprehensions by normalizing the thesis production process. Researchers routinely start ... and then routinely finish. Moreover, after completion there is immediately a new and quite different challenge: to present the research findings to the wider world (on which see chapter 18). Thus each ending can become another beginning ...

17. Experiencing the viva

SIGNPOST: Relevant for researchers studying for a higher degree which requires a formal interview known as the viva; also contains advice on interview preparation and presentation which is relevant to all researchers.

Savouring the moment of crossing the finishing line.

17.1 The big interview

The focus here is upon the sequential stages of anticipation, participation and learning from a big viva examination at the end of a doctoral programme.[1] A number of general principles apply – and they can, moreover, be adopted for many parallel cases, such as job interviews, where questions will invariably be asked about original research.

---

[1] R. Murray, *How to Survive Your Viva: Defending a Thesis in an Oral Examination* (Maidenhead, 2009); V. Trafford and S. Leshem, *Stepping Stones to Achieving Your Doctorate: Focusing on Your Viva from the Start* (Maidenhead, 2008).

As in any moment of purposive communication, it is important to think not only of pinpointing one's own big message but simultaneously of making the message fully comprehensible to others. The race to the finishing tape is not waged against any immediate rival in an adjacent lane. It is a solo test. Yet there are race stewards in the form of the examiners, who have the final responsibility of deciding upon a Pass or other alternatives (outlined in section 17.7). In effect, they are deciding whether the campaign to become a historian has succeeded.

Therefore candidates before the interview should aim to be ready with the fine mixture of intense exhilaration and inner calm that top athletes strive to feel at the starting tape.

17.2 Anticipation

Everything that has been discovered, debated and written during the doctoral programme has been in preparation for a final public advocacy in the form of a viva. Hence, in the most obvious way, candidates are already prepared. However, it's good to anticipate specifically what such an interview will entail.

Before the meeting, examiners will have read the thesis in detail and made a preliminary report, with a provisional recommendation. They are entitled, however, to upgrade (but not downgrade) their verdict in the light of the viva performance. The 'live' encounter thus remains crucial. These days it's very common for the examiners to start by asking the candidate to give a succinct statement of the research aims and outcomes. It's wise therefore to have a pithy account prepared and ready. It provides a great chance to set the terms of the ensuing discussion. And even if the examiners don't begin with such a request, it often happens that having such a summary to hand is really helpful.

Before producing an opening statement, it's essential to reread the thesis or research project in its entirety. It's particularly important to refresh one's thoughts if there has been a long gap in time between submission of the thesis and the date of the viva. (These days, there are strict time limits; but even so, sometimes there are unavoidable delays.) When preparing the summary statement, it's useful, at the same time, to note, calmly and judiciously, the good points of the study – and then to consider, equally calmly and judiciously, where criticisms and challenges might be made. Some authors deeply love everything that they have written; others detest their own prose. A sensible balance works best.

Having noted areas for criticism and challenge, it's then the moment to think carefully about the best answers to such criticisms. It's not invariably true that authors are their own best critics. Nonetheless, they can often tell where the shoe pinches. Supervisors or mentors will also help with this process.

Most research students will already have had practice at being interviewed on their work, in the form of the progression or upgrade viva – and quite possibly by giving a seminar paper as well. Such occasions are invaluable. Anyone feeling rusty and uncertain should ask the research supervisor to arrange another practice session. And those who have not previously had such an experience should immediately take steps to gain it. If nothing more formalized is available, even a session of talking to a circle of interested friends is helpful, to gain practice in introducing the main research themes and findings, explaining why they are interesting and important, and answering questions. Of course, there is a nice balance to find between preparation and over-anxiety. The aim, as already noted, is to be ready but simultaneously not agitated.

17.3 The status of the viva

Everywhere, the final vetting of a doctoral thesis is a serious matter. But the formal role of the viva is a matter of some variation between different national academic traditions. Those differences have evolved historically – but are tending to become reduced with the international pooling of qualifications.

In the UK, the viva remains a big pass/fail hurdle. It is conducted in closed session, usually lasting for one and a half or (more commonly) two hours. By contrast, in France the viva is an impressive public event, continuing for some hours, at which candidates are put through their intellectual paces by an august jury of experienced academics. Friends, families and any interested members of the general public are entitled to attend, and many do. In those circumstances, however, the critical vetting has been done beforehand. Hence candidates in France who have failed are not called for a public viva, which, while a challenging event, is a confirmation of success.

Closed vivas play a different, more pedagogic role. They are oral examinations, not public showcases. It is thus not appropriate to invite family and friends to wait immediately outside the room where the viva is being conducted. After the session has ended, all parties need a period of quiet reflection. The examiners may not have announced their verdict immediately – and may ask the candidate to wait outside while they confer. It's also vital for researchers and supervisors to have a quick debriefing after the viva, and to check on the timetable for corrections and revisions, if any are required. All in all, vivas are tiring occasions, and some time to rest and recover is helpful. Therefore friends and family are best invited to celebrate later in the day – or even on another day entirely.

One protocol which applies in all examination systems is an obvious point of etiquette – but one which bears repeating. Candidates must *not* attempt to contact or to influence the examiners either directly or indirectly; or to offer a gift or any inducement that might distract them from their academic judgement. Equally obviously, the doctoral research and writing has to be the fruit of the individual historian's own authentic work. There is a deplorable and semi-hidden world of bogus scholarship and fake credentials.[2] Shady businesses offer, for a fee, to engage expert strangers to write essays and dissertations for candidates who lack confidence in their own abilities. The doctorate, however, remains a gold standard among degrees. One key function of the viva – whether a public event or closed session – is thus to enable candidates to 'own' their big research projects 'live' in front of experts. It is a solemn event, because it constitutes the culmination and celebration of great effort.

17.4 Participation

Candidates, who are coming to share their ideas with fellow scholars who are appointed as examiners, should not be obsequious or deferential. The viva is a high-powered research consultancy, where all parties are invited to confer on a substantive piece of research. Hence, it is a mistake, equally, for candidates to display *either* too much swagger (off-putting) *or* too much fear (disappointing). In practical terms, dress should be comfortable but not distracting. And body language should signal keen interest throughout. Candidates should thus maintain suitable eye contact with the examiners, while refraining entirely from using mobile phones.

These days, vivas are always conducted in a serious and professional way. They are intense affairs (as are job interviews). As a result, candidates often don't remember much of the discussion. Some indeed may experience a sharp headache afterwards – often followed by a surge of euphoria, if all has gone well. Those candidates who have the option of inviting the supervisor to attend the viva (not all universities allow this practice) should accept. It provides a friendly witness. The supervisors are not, in most systems, the examiners. And they are not invited to intervene in the procedures. Instead, they sit silently to one side while keeping useful notes.

---

[2] Universities, governments and employers worldwide share an interest in detecting and, ideally, halting the spread of fake qualifications. See L. J. Børresen and S. A. Skierven, 'Detecting fake university degrees in a digital world', *University World News*, 14 Sept. 2018: <https://www.universityworldnews.com/post.php?story=20180911120249317> [accessed 30 April 2021].

Hence, after the viva, they can advise candidates on how to implement the examiners' recommendations.

Most of the meeting is taken up by a prolonged and detailed discussion. It covers points both small and large, in something of a barrage. The researcher's task is to assess the commentary and/or questions, and then to take an instant decision. If the points raised are crucial to the core message, then it's vital to stand firm, courteously but decisively, and defend the case. The viva, after all, is a core test. If, on the other hand, the criticisms are well made and are not absolutely central, then it's fine to give way graciously and promise to amend either in a revised thesis or in a subsequent publication. Every moment requires a quick assessment and a suitable response. Candidates are on the spot throughout, which is why vivas are experienced as both exciting and tiring.

Either at the very start of the session (less common these days) or at the very end (becoming the usual practice), the examiners state their verdict. But candidates should put that thought out of their minds. The important thing is to concentrate on the discussion. And nothing but the discussion.

Above all, it's vital to remember that the examiners have not been asked whether they warm to the candidate; or even whether they agree personally with the core argument and conclusions in a doctoral thesis. Their task is a straightforwardly professional one. Examiners in a history viva are asked to assess whether the thesis has made an original contribution to historical knowledge, which is well argued, well documented and presented to a publishable standard. No more, and no less. The candidate's task is therefore to concentrate upon fielding their comments/questions and to *keep the ball in play*. By the way, that maxim provides sound advice for all interviewees everywhere.

17.5 Outcomes

As already noted, it was once more common for examiners to announce their verdict at the very start of the viva. Generally, however, it is considered best to give the candidates a good intellectual workout – and that process is best served by debating in a state of excited suspense. At the end, the examiners may simply confer quickly by a mutual nod of the head. In that case, they can make an immediate announcement. At other times, they ask the candidate to withdraw while they cogitate. The examiners may also make specific suggestions for publication, though they are not required to do so.

Whatever then happens, the best advice for all candidates is to greet the verdict from the examiners with good grace and to extract as positive a result as possible, even in the event of bad news. There are many gradations of results, between Pass with no corrections and Fail without the option of resubmitting. (See list in section 17.7, with suggested responses.) Often there are corrections to be made, whether major or minor. The advice of supervisors is always very helpful at this stage. And then it's advisable to make corrections as rapidly as possible, to profit from the examiners' input and to keep momentum.

If, however, there are valid concerns over the conduct of a doctoral viva, it is open to candidates to contest the verdict on procedural grounds. There is always an appeals system. Candidates who are seriously unhappy should immediately write down notes on what went wrong. They should also consult the supervisor, who, if in attendance at the viva, constitutes a crucial witness. And then they can appeal. However, it's notable that challenges to PhD vivas are very rare; and rarely successful, unless a university has seriously failed to follow its own rules. That's because, in this age of accountability, examinations are generally conducted with great care, by the book.

Obviously, it's best to prepare for success. But, if seriously disappointed, then it's always worth considering what other uses can be made of the research data – for example, in some form of a publication or web presentation. These days there are many diverse outlets. If the journey on the official trackway should hit the buffers, it's worth seeking positive alternatives instead.

17.6 Summary: progression into the wider world

Passing the viva or finishing a big independently authored research project is a real *rite de passage*. Researchers are no longer apprentices but have submitted their master-work. (That masculine term is understood in this context to be applicable to all genders.) Successful candidates have joined the ranks of the experienced scholars. A doctorate is a known heavyweight qualification which is admired by academics worldwide as well as generally respected by the wider public. After the results of the viva are declared, it's definitely time for a deep breath and some suitable celebration. Sadly, most places in the world do not follow the Finnish tradition of presenting a ceremonial sword to successful doctoral candidates. Nonetheless, the achievement is real everywhere. And the exciting next step, as explained in chapter 18, is to tell the wider world.

17.7 Note on the range of viva outcomes (subject to variation between different institutions) and appropriate responses

Pass with award of PhD (or DPhil in Oxbridge nomenclature), with absolutely no changes required.
[Excellent. NB: This verdict is very unusual, as there are often a few minor editing points which require clarification/amendment/correction.]

Pass with award of PhD, subject to minor corrections required within a short period, often three months.
[Very good. The most common result. In response, the required corrections, often seeking clarification or additional documentation, should be made with due care but as much speed as possible.]

Pass with PhD, subject to substantial corrections to rectify errors of substance or omission, to be completed within longer period, usually nine months.
[This verdict gives encouragement that, once the required substantial corrections are made, the thesis will eventually be passed – after a further check, usually undertaken by one designated examiner. There is a question as to how 'major' these substantial corrections can be. Examiners cannot ask a candidate to change the core argument of a thesis. But they are entitled to ask for substantial remedial work if the evidence is thin, or poorly presented, or poorly integrated into the general discussion. In such circumstances, candidates should not despair. But they should talk frankly with the supervisor, who will assist in timetabling further research and rewriting within the specified time.]

Reference back, allowing resubmission for PhD, with considerable corrections required within eighteen months, with or without a second viva, with no guarantee that revised version will be passed.
[Initially a very disappointing verdict; but, viewed in the right light, it gives a chance to make the required improvements/corrections and to head off substantial criticisms before the thesis becomes public. Again – candidates should talk things through with the supervisor, and get to work.]

Pass with MPhil – i.e. degree awarded at lower academic level.
[Certainly disappointing; and comparatively rare. Once recovering from the shock, the best response is to be pleased to have gained a valid research qualification, even if not the one desired. It is always possible to challenge the examiners' decision, but supervisors should be consulted before taking such a step. Certainly big decisions should not be rushed in the shadow of disappointment. There's no point in wasting time pursuing a will o' the wisp if there is little chance of making a successful objection.]

Pass with MPhil, subject to either minor or major corrections, to be completed within specified number of months.
[The previous advice applies; candidates should grit their teeth and make the required changes.]

Resubmit for MPhil, with substantial corrections, to be completed within twelve months, with no guarantee that revised version will be passed.

[The previous advice applies, with additional gritting of teeth.]

Fail outright, for both PhD and MPhil, without chance of revising and resubmitting.

[This drastic outcome should not happen, as internal departmental or faculty review processes should have halted the candidacy before getting to the viva. In the rare event of outright failure, candidates should reassess in consultation with the supervisor, and consider what alternative outcomes, including publications and/or web presentations, can be achieved with the research material.]

18. Moving on to publication and civic engagement

SIGNPOST: Relevant to all researchers

And the next stage is to tell the world by every means at hand: well-researched historical studies are always in demand.

18.1 Historians and outreach

It's going far too far to claim that, for all those newly awarded their history doctorates, the world is their oyster. The jobs market, especially for academic posts, is everywhere uncertain and insecure. And there are conflicting cultural currents today – some admiring and appreciating effort and achievements; some sceptical about all forms of 'experts'. Nonetheless, history researchers with a doctorate have a massive qualification to list on their CVs. They have hard-won skills and knowledge to communicate. And they deal in a subject of universal interest. Even those who claim to dislike the subject of history, often thinking of 'boring' textbooks from their youth, turn out to have some interests beyond the here and now. All are located in Time.

Given the universalism of the subject, it's really rare to find any historical theme that cannot command some interest in the wider community. For that reason, there's every reason for researchers immediately post-doc to proceed rapidly to a first publication (whether a book or an article), arising out of their studies. Most supervisors are happy to help with further advice; and the doctoral examiners probably gave relevant suggestions too.

Furthermore, there are other options to be followed in tandem. These include various forms of civic engagement, which are known, rather cheerily, as 'outreach'. That terminology is not perfect. It conjures up images of a secluded academic ivory tower, from which secluded scholars stretch out their arms to a startled public. Nonetheless, 'outreach' is the current term of art for scholarly links with the wider community. And the process of civic engagement is well worthwhile for all historians, whatever the terminology.

18.2 Preparing for publication

Getting into print for the first time is a good moment. Most historian-authors are delighted. Some indeed say that they don't believe in their research until they see it in print. Only a tiny number positively dislike the experience. Friends and family are also relieved that there's something to show for all those years of labour. Employers are almost invariably impressed with a publication. And, above all, appearing in print, after a due process of pre-publication scrutiny, gives historical research a public *imprimatur*: a badge of research honour. Crossing the bridge into print – and thereby into the scholarly community – used to be comparatively difficult. These days, there are multiple opportunities to issue public communications. Nonetheless, the value of appearing in a peer-reviewed outlet has not diminished. It conveys both serious intent and scholarly acceptance. It allows readers to access the work, triggering responses and debates. And it may well launch researchers into further publications, having taken the plunge.

Immediately after gaining a doctorate or completing a large research project, it is worth pondering the options. Are there spin-off essays which can be ready relatively quickly? Is there a suitable target journal or other media outlet? But it's a mistake to dissipate the impact of a big study by spreading the word in too many short essays. Publishers have been known to reject book plans on the reasonable grounds that the material is already in the public domain. Strategic thought is thus advisable.

Scholarly outputs range from a research monograph to overview books, edited documents with scholarly commentaries, spin-off surveys, detailed research essays, research blogs and web publications, *ad infinitum*. It's up to each individual researcher to decide which trackway is most appropriate.[1]

However, it's worth remembering that, for formal research assessment purposes, publications have to pass a process of anonymous peer review. It can seem annoying, particularly after the hard work to get a doctorate, that a spin-off book or essays are subject to yet more assessment. But that's what the world of scholarship requires. The anonymous peer-review process applies to new authors and old hands alike. It's a process of pre-publication checking, which patrols the boundary between the world of scholarship and the unchecked torrent of writings on anything/everything else.

When critical responses arrive from the anonymous experts, researchers are sometimes startled or even offended. There's something about anonymity which causes referees to be brisk, brusque and occasionally rude. The aggression expressed by so many anonymous authors on social media illustrates that syndrome only too effectively.[2] Yet a dose of well-founded academic criticism can often be salutary. So, after recovering from the initial shock, researchers should view the exercise as a further free consultation. Instead of rushing into print and getting a stinker of a review, the author is being forewarned. The anonymous critic is, in fact, a best friend lurking in disguise (another variant of the hostile questioner after a seminar presentation).

Accordingly, it's best to grit one's teeth – and to adapt and/or polish in the light of criticisms. Often, rewriting helps to strengthen arguments. Obscure references can be clarified; sloppy analysis tightened; and contrary views acknowledged before being rebutted.

Nonetheless, there are times when the criticisms have to be rejected. In such circumstances, researchers should send a courteous explanation to the relevant publisher or editor. They need to know that the would-be author is not acting capriciously, but has a good reason for rejecting the anonymous advice. Once reassured on that point, publishers/editors often, but not invariably, allow the publication to go ahead. It's their judgement call, as they weigh up the options between either sticking cautiously with established experts or trusting the reassurances from a new author. But the review process means that publishers/editors have reasoned evidence to consult before deciding. It's another stage of negotiation.

---

[1] J. Coverdale et al., *Writing for Academia: Getting Your Research into Print* (Dundee, 2014); G. Wisker, *Getting Published: Academic Publishing Success* (London, 2017).

[2] See G. M. Chen, *Online Incivility and Public Debate: Nasty Talk* (London, 2017); W. Phillips, *This Is Why We Can't Have Nice Things: Mapping the Relationship between Online Trolling and Mainstream Culture* (Cambridge, Mass., 2015).

There is kudos to be gained from appearing with high-rated publishing houses, so authors should be ambitious. At the same time, all interests have to be served. If one publisher wants to change a project out of all recognition, then authors are better advised to look elsewhere.

After a book or essay has been given the green light, the publication process starts. It can at times be painfully slow. The processes of book designing, formatting, copy-editing, proofreading (often twice), indexing, printing and promoting cannot be done in a day, though it's true that some publishers manage to take fewer days than others. All this effort, however, is worth it when a fine-quality publication ensues.

18.3 Publication outlets

Getting into print requires would-be authors to be pro-active. It is not the same as being an examination candidate, when the vetting process is organized by others. However, publishing is usually populated by people who are keenly interested in the world of ideas. So newcomers are readily encouraged. Most publishers provide forms which ask for information about the proposed book's length, structure and import, as well as information about its place in the market and the nature of competitor works.

Shorter essays, meanwhile, may be destined for academic journals. All material submitted for consideration should have been scrupulously prepared in the required house-style, as editors usually return sloppy work unread. It is worth noting that the long-term survival of these publications remains unclear, as new policies of open access for publicly funded research projects are changing the terms of trade. Nonetheless, dedicated editors of academic journals usually have a strong commitment to fostering their field of study. Otherwise, they wouldn't undertake what is normally a part-time, unpaid task. Hence they are generally delighted to get contributions, especially from early career scholars. It marks a welcome renewal of the field.

Academic book publishers, meanwhile, are more varied. A number are fairly conservative. But others are genuinely adventurous. They love the world of ideas and are keen to engage with the public. Older historians who have already published will give advice and recommendations, both positive and negative. Personal contacts are always useful, not in hopes of great financial rewards, since academic publishing is not lucrative, but for professional input. Great publishers nurture their fields – and historians who find such paragons are lucky.

A few academics who hope for significant pecuniary rewards employ literary agents. These are usually delightful people, full of news of books, markets, financial advances and gossip. Yet it should be noted that only the most commercially attractive of topics earn sufficient money to make it worth employing a go-between who takes a cut of the normally derisory profits. And, of course, not all of these 'trade books', as they are termed, do actually have runaway sales. There are flops as well as successes. Indeed, very few, even among the most popular 'trade' books, make money (for the author at least) from publishing alone.

As a result, most research historians deal directly with publishers, whose standard offers are very modest. The reality is that most academic publications have limited print-runs, many as low as 250 to 300 copies. Morcover, the modest payments to authors don't reflect the huge effort it takes to produce a learned monograph of 100,000+ words. It is the employing institutions (often, the universities) which pay the salaries that enable so much professional research and writing to be completed. Hence, the academic sector within publishing is subsidized.

However, the relationship is a symbiotic one. Academic publishing permits specialist works with only limited markets to appear in print, to the satisfaction of universities and research institutions. Ever-conscious of their rankings, these institutions strongly pressurize their staff to publish. For that reason, a blind eye has long been turned to the low market-valuation of the academic contribution to publishing, whether in terms of research, authorship, editorial input, quality control or quantities of time.

Currently, however, the terms of trade are changing, with the result that some businesses are getting authors to organize and pay for tasks – such as copy-editing, indexing and securing copyright permission for use of images – which were once undertaken by publishers. It's a real dilemma for researchers. In effect, some academics are being pushed not just into publishing for a pittance but into publishing at their own expense.

Moreover, current debates over open access for materials in peer-reviewed journals are further complicating the knotty question of who precisely should bear or share the true costs of essays in academic journals: researchers? research funders? institutions? institutional funders? publishers? libraries?[3]

In such circumstances, the option of self-publication is becoming increasingly attractive. Essays can be published readily on the web. And larger projects can be produced as attractive books either by professional businesses, who undertake the task for a fee, or by determined individuals who manage to self-publish to professional standards.[4]

---

[3] T. Rabesandratana, 'The world debates open-access mandates', *Science*, ccclxiii (2019), 11–12, and extensive review in <https://en.wikipedia.org/wiki/Open_access> [accessed 30 April 2021].

[4] For independent publishing of impeccable quality, see the already cited Bird (ed.), *Diary of Mary Hardy, 1733–1809.*

Consequently, researchers can and do explore the entire gamut of outlets. Ultimately, however, it depends upon what is wanted. For money and fame, works on historical sex, scandal, witchcraft, world wars, Hitler, Stalin and the Tudor monarchs all offer tempting possibilities with a commercial press. Or, for instant action, self-publication cuts out the intermediary assessment and the delays.

Yet there remains a large area in between. It's the journal editors and academic publishers who open the doors to the scholarly arena. They not only provide worldwide distribution networks, which self-publishers do not enjoy, but they also offer a guarantee of scholarly validity via the authentication of peer review before publication.

The best advice is to take the plunge, via whichever outlet appears most suitable. All books and essays have the potential to throw off further sparks, which potentially generate further reviews, debates, conference sessions, replies and rebuttals/restatements. All exciting and energizing. And even works which do not generate immediate responses (reviews can be slow to appear) have nonetheless placed their arguments fair and square in the public arena.

18.4 Civic engagement

Historians are always in much demand. They are consulted by everyone from governments and diplomats to film-makers and advertising gurus. They provide bedrock advice and information for the massive heritage industries.[5] And today the pressures upon historians to undertake all forms of civic engagement are multiplying. The major problem is time. As careers burgeon, so do the number of tasks requiring attention.

But, without teams of support staff, individual historians cannot be simultaneously working in the archives, giving public talks, writing grant applications, curating exhibitions, organizing conferences, reviewing books, writing peer reviews, teaching, marking essays, setting exam papers, appearing on social media, making videos, organizing 'witness' history projects in the local community, keeping up to date in their administration, producing a regular flow of research articles and, of course, writing their books.

The obvious response is a degree of specialization. No-one should try to do everything. Some work will always remain 'back-room', supporting

[5] D. Armitage and J. Guldi, *The History Manifesto* (Cambridge, 2014); J. de Groot, *Consuming History: Historians and Heritage in Contemporary Popular Culture* (London, 2016); M. Finn and K. Smith (ed.), *New Paths to Public Histories* (Basingstoke, 2015); S. Berger (ed.), *Perspectives on the Intersection between Politics, Activism and the Historical Profession* (New York, 2019); J. L. Koslow, *Public History: an Introduction* (London, 2021).

teaching and underpinning the knowledge grid. Tasks should be shared within departments and faculties, and individual researchers encouraged to link their projects (such as giving talks or organizing exhibitions on themes closely related to their latest research), so that they do not spread themselves too thin. It's also worth recalling that people work most enthusiastically at projects that they really want to undertake. 'Outreach' commitments should therefore be tailored to the individual researcher's aptitudes and preferences.

One common form of engagement for historians is giving formal lectures and informal talks on a huge variety of historical themes. Invitations come from student societies, local history groups, the Historical Association, Universities of the Third Age, heritage and literary festivals, and so on. Often speakers at these events are unpaid or given no more than a token honorarium, plus travel expenses. But audiences like to hear about the variety of research, and it's a good challenge for researchers to talk to audiences who have no preconceptions and who frequently respond with sharp comments and perceptive criticisms.

Providing ideas and historical briefings for TV and radio gurus, and for film-makers, is another big area for historians – depending upon the nature of individual research specialisms. Exchanges with such communicators can be very zippy. And at times annoying. Media people tend to demand instant attention, which is not always convenient. And some have fixed ideas on a subject, which they are reluctant to change even after seeking professional advice. The consultancy process is thus dialogic and sometimes a bit edgy. But it's generally worth the effort.

By the way, a percentage of such consultancies are unpaid, being part of the free exchange of ideas. However, historians should not let themselves be pushed inadvertently into acting as unpaid research assistants. If the hours of work are great – and the borrowing of ideas extensive – then researchers are entitled to ask for due recognition in the credits and at least a minimal fee to acknowledge the input of time and professional labour.

'Public' historians, who undertake a lot of civic engagements, quickly gain expertise in the different media of communication. In radio interviews, for example, the answers should be 'front-loaded'. That is, the verdict should come briskly at the start, with the complications explained afterwards. The contrast with a long lecture is notable. Thus, while it's fine to start an hour-long talk by observing that the question is complex, such an observation merely sounds evasive if given as a reply to a radio interviewer. Another significant variation relates to the use of sound and silence. In a long lecture, a significant pause can have a dramatic effect. But radio producers hate silences. They fear losing their listeners' attention. Hence speakers trying to add variety into their presentations should do so with words, not with meaningful silences. Radio-talk is a stylization of face-to-face speech, not a direct replica. It's performative, even if not every intervention has to be a full-blown 'performance'.[6]

Communication by TV, film or video has another different set of imperatives. This medium needs a flow of images even more than a flow of sound. The input from human communicators should be engaging but not in any way distracting. Hence historians on screen should resolve not to fidget; not to wave their hands in the air; not to look directly at the people operating the camera, the mike, the sound baffle and so forth; and certainly not to seek responses from the technical staff. They are not the audience, and are trained to be impassive. The audience is the other side of the camera, far away. Their attention may lapse if the flow of images is insufficiently interesting.[7] Hence advisors for historical film, video and so forth need to think of ways of representing ideas in a manner that is neither too bland and obvious nor too baffling and obscure. A great challenge.

Collectively, these forms of civic engagement are viewed today as part of the Impact Agenda.[8] It seeks to measure the value of research in terms of its contribution to the UK's economy, society and culture, preferably in quantifiable form. A fine example would be an exhibition to display new findings, with attendance figures which can be tallied and visitors' comments – usually appreciative from those who have made an effort to attend – logged.

There is clearly a positive side to the Impact Agenda. Reports of such productive activities help governments to justify expenditure on higher education. Nonetheless, an exaggerated stress upon 'impact' could damage the breadth of research. Its focus is very much upon the assessable short term.[9] But some projects have impact only in the long run. And others simply

---

[6] C. B. Cooney, *The Voice on the Radio* (London, 1996); D. Crider, *Performing Personality: On-Air Radio Identities in a Changing Media Landscape* (Lanham, Md., 2016); S. VanCour, *Making Radio: Early Radio Production and the Rise of Modern Sound Culture* (New York, 2018).

[7] Making a lengthy video provides a quick education in the differences between preparing an illustrated lecture and finding an unbroken flow of images for a prolonged exposition.

[8] See *The Research Excellence Framework: Diversity, Collaboration, Impact Criteria, and Preparing for Open Access* (Westminster, 2019): British Library online resource no. 019466976.

[9] B. R. Martin, 'The Research Excellence Framework and the "impact agenda": are we creating a Frankenstein monster?', *Research Evaluation*, xx (Sept. 2011), 247–54, and other contributions in the same issue; R. Watermeyer, *Competitive Accountability in Academic*

contribute to good up-to-date teaching and extending the knowledge grid, without glitzy spin-offs.

No doubt, however, a balance will in time emerge. Researchers into unfashionable subjects should hold their nerve, while those with material that attracts public interest should enjoy the civic engagement while it lasts. History springs enough surprises to suggest that the current parameters of academic research assessment are unlikely to remain set in stone.

18.5 Summary: public sparks and inner fires

Ideas and knowledge, once in print and/or in wider circulation, have a chequered history. They make public sparks whose illumination spreads well beyond the control of their originators, whether new research is forgotten, or contradicted, or quietly assimilated, or loudly applauded. In the world of knowledge, effective outcomes are assessed not in a few months or years but over generations.

There are instances of books which fall completely flat at first publication but eventually become foundational. David Hume's *Treatise on Human Nature*, which in 1738, in his wry phrase, 'fell dead-born from the press', is the paradigm case.[10] It is still in print today with rival editions vying for readers' attention. And the reverse can happen too. There are plenty of once-notable but now forgotten authors.[11] And there have been influential historians of global renown in one generation whose fame plummets in the next. It happened to Arnold Toynbee, whose panoramic style of world history, much praised in the 1950s, went abruptly out of fashion in the 1960s.[12]

So what is the moral for today's researchers? Only time will provide the ultimate assessment. In the meantime, historians should warm themselves not only by the sparky processes of publication and civic engagement – but simultaneously by their own inner fires.

Life: the Struggle for Social Impact and Public Legitimacy (Cheltenham, 2019); K. Smith et al., *The Impact Agenda: Controversies, Consequences and Challenges* (Bristol, 2020).

[10] A. Bailey and D. O'Brien (ed.), *The Continuum Companion to Hume* (New York, 2012); P. Russell, *The Riddle of Hume's Treatise: Scepticism, Naturalism and Irreligion* (Oxford, 2008).

[11] C. Fowler, *The Book of Forgotten Authors* (London, 2017).

[12] For Arnold J. Toynbee, contrast views in C. T. McIntire and M. Perry (ed.), *Toynbee: Reappraisals* (Toronto, 1989); K. Winetrout (ed.), *After One Is Dead: Arnold Toynbee as Prophet – Essays in Honour of Toynbee's Centennial* (Hampden, Mass., 1989); and M. Perry, *Arnold Toynbee and the Western Tradition* (New York, 1996).

PART IV
Taking the long view – career outcomes

19. Academic and parallel trackways

SIGNPOST: Discussion of academic trackways is relevant to those seeking academic posts; discussion of parallel career trackways is relevant to all researchers.

The multifarious trackways open to historians, whose skills and knowledge last a lifetime.

At the end of a doctorate or any extended research project, individual researchers know their own topics – however large or small – better than anyone. It took time in the UK and elsewhere for this qualification to become fully appreciated.[1] Yet it is now an unquestioned scholarly accolade. All successful candidates have become world experts in their fields. And with that expertise has come an enviable range of additional skills. Organizing data, writing clearly and accurately, turning complexity into sense, knowing how to manage a project that takes years to complete: these are capacities that are in perennial demand in all walks of life.

19.1 Academic trackways

Many researchers begin a history doctorate with the assumption that it will lead to an academic career. But frequently this outcome is not realized. In part, it is the natural corollary of the difficult truth that many more people gain doctorates in history every year than there are lectureships in the field. And that proposition holds true even before the presence of international candidates is factored into the equation.

All good supervisors will have sought to make prospective students aware of just how difficult the academic job market can be before they commit to four or more years of further study. However, in the excitement of beginning, this frank advice is not always fully registered.

As a result, many excellent scholars find themselves, after completing the degree, applying unsuccessfully for post-doctoral positions or undertaking temporary teaching contracts. Many experience the real frustrations of 'precarity'.[2] This state of affairs does not reflect the quality of their work. The standard for a doctorate is an 'original contribution to knowledge', and that accolade is about as high as it gets. Yet the hard reality is that many more people wish to work as university lecturers than there are positions to fill.

There are also issues beyond any individual's control which ensure that there is no straightforward path to an academic career. Areas of study fall into and out of fashion; and the curriculum changes in complex ways, following both academic fashions and also in response to the demands and expectations of wider society. As a result, job descriptions change; and great research projects don't always fit.

[1] R. Simpson, *How the PhD Came to Britain: a Century of Struggle for Postgraduate Education* (Guildford, 1983).

[2] G. Standing, *The Precariat: the New Dangerous Class* (London, 2016); J.-A. Johannessen, *The Workplace of the Future: the Fourth Industrial Revolution, the Precariat and the Death of Hierarchies* (London, 2018); T. Zaniello, *The Cinema of the Precariat: the Exploited, Underemployed and Temp Workers of the World* (New York, 2020).

Moreover, while a doctorate these days is a necessary requirement for employment as a university lecturer, it is not a sufficient one. Most university jobs are built around teaching, and involve a large component of administration, as well as research and writing. There have also been deplorable forms of discrimination at times in the past against specific candidates, whether in terms of religion, gender, sexuality or ethnic heritage. Any traditional prejudices should be fast disappearing, but it is incumbent upon all historians, as all good citizens, to encourage a spirit of openness and egalitarian welcome, and to combat systematic discrimination, whenever and wherever detected.

Such considerations should not discourage anyone from undertaking a research degree. Yet (to repeat) it is essential to realize from the outset that it provides no guarantee of an academic career. It's best to regard the experience of advanced research as a good in itself. Successfully undertaken, it provides the highest academic qualification attainable – which constitutes a standout feature on any CV.

Gaining a history doctorate thus supplies the basis for a possible academic career.[3] And it simultaneously opens doors to many parallel forms of employment, given a readiness to embrace flexibility. In sum, while a doctorate confers no entitlement, it carries with it immense potential.

19.2 Parallel trackways

It's never a surprise, therefore, to find advanced history graduates in even the most recondite and amazing occupations. They find jobs everywhere: in the army; the navy; the police; sports; nursing; catering; all the creative arts; journalism; social media; film-making; publishing; business; finance; marketing; consultancy; the trade unions; social work; computing; the intelligence services; law; politics; administration and the churches.

Systematic studies of the employment trackways of all history graduates, among whom postgraduates form an advanced sub-set, have confirmed the immense diversity of their careers.[4] Today, advice networks provide

---

[3] Books don't sell by setting their claims too low: see I. Hay, *How to Be an Academic Superhero: Establishing and Sustaining a Successful Career in the Social Sciences, Arts and Humanities* (Cheltenham, 2017).

[4] D. Nicholls, *The Employment of History Graduates: a Report for the Higher Education Authority Subject Centre for History, Classics, Archaeology* (London, 2005): <https://www.advance-he.ac.uk/knowledge-hub/employment-history-graduates> [accessed 30 April 2021]; D. Nicholls, *The Employment of History Graduates: Update* (London, 2011): <https://warwick.ac.uk/fac/cross_fac/heahistory/research/gwi/emp_report> [accessed 30 April 2021]; and spin-off in D. Nicholls, 'Famous history graduates', *History Today*, lii (2002), 49–51.

encouragement in the same vein. They urge all humanities researchers with doctorates to aim high but also to cast their nets widely.[5]

Meanwhile, significant instances of people with history doctorates can be found working in administration (including university management); the intelligence services; politics;[6] political consultancies; TV and radio; libraries; museums; archives; teaching at all levels; and freelance writing.

One graduate with a PhD in art history is the American Allison Harbin. After a spell in academe, she turned to high-school teaching plus freelance writing and civic campaigning, challenging corruption and racism in education. Her time in grad school, she muses, provided excellent preparation for her multi-track working life in a precarious world.[7]

This specific trackway is far from a typical one, except in its versatility. Yet that key quality is entirely compatible with an apprenticeship as a historian. It points not just to one career destination but, on the contrary, opens doors to the world.

19.3 Summary: trained historians' knowledge and skills

Collectively, people trained as historians have skills *and* knowledge. Or the point can be put the other way round. Historians have deep knowledge which is based upon deep skills. They know about the past and its links to the present. They can think both micro and macro. They understand the benefits of comparative approaches.

Above all, they are not worried by complexity but rather expect to assess its intricacies. Historians therefore have reservoirs of understanding, and do not immediately rush to explain things in the light of the latest bright idea or intellectual fashion. They understand the uses of empathy for people in the past and how that differs from – though it may overlap with – sympathy. And then they are trained to find and assess large quantities of data; to organize the material into coherent arguments, complete with full referencing; and to locate their interpretations within a bigger picture.

In sum, those who have become historians have gained multiple skills *plus* deep knowledge: great human attributes which are readily applicable in many different contexts – and which last a lifetime.

---

[5] See 'Ten career opportunities for Humanities PhDs': <https://cheekyscientist.com /career-opportunities-for-humanities-phds> [accessed 30 April 2021].

[6] Three eminent politicians with history doctorates are the USA's State Senator Daniel Patrick Moynihan (senator for New York, 1977–2001); the UK's Gordon Brown (prime minister, 2007–10); and Iceland's Guðni Thorlacius Jóhannesson (president, 2016–).

[7] A. Harbin, 'It gets better: PhD to freelance writer': <https://www.allisonharbin.com /post-phd/it-gets-better> [accessed 3 April 2021].

PART V
Reflecting

20. Retrospective thoughts

SIGNPOST: Ending the journey together

20.1 From PJC

Co-writing is an instructive experience. Among many things, it teaches the value of comparing rival perspectives. Tim Hitchcock and I agree on our deepest and most fundamental objectives. Yet we disagree about the pace of change. Tim Hitchcock (who switched country and culture when moving from the USA to study for an Oxford doctorate) maintains a comparative outsider's view of the British university scene. He tends to see the sclerosis of slow change.

By contrast, as someone more familiar with the system, I see it as pluralist and diversified. It has areas of deep traditionalism but also areas of innovation. It has room for experimentation in courses and teaching styles. In the twentieth century, moreover, the British system began to admit (in sequence) working-class men, women and people of diverse heritage. Further democratization is still needed. And not all innovations are beneficial. Yet systems are open to change, both in the UK and worldwide.

Balancing my relative optimism with Tim Hitchcock's critical impatience generated keen debates between us. The outcome has improved this *Guide*. It requires a good mix of hope and haste to demystify the world of historical research – and to invite all comers to join.

20.2 From TH

History is a community project. There may be scholars out there who sit alone in an archive and are happy in their isolation, but most of us crave an audience for our work, and a conversation.

This book has been created as a conversation between Penelope Corfield and myself. As she mentions, we often disagreed; but, as I don't agree with any of my best friends about much, that struck me as a good thing! And I believe this volume is better for it. The resulting confection combines my rather jaundiced and occasionally cynical view of the historical profession in the UK with Penelope Corfield's infectious enthusiasm and sheer intellectual joy at the wonder of research and writing. The combination creates a more balanced introduction than either of us could create on our own.

This book has also been a conversation of a different sort, with all the thousands of researchers who have attended University of London's seminar on British History in the Long Eighteenth Century over the last four decades. For both of us, I believe the seminar forms an intellectual home, and the primary site of our shared academic community. And in the writing, the voices of all those friends and interlocutors have been whispering in my ear.

Select reading list

General guides

J. M. Banner, *Being a Historian: an Introduction to the Professional World of History* (Cambridge, 2012)

J. Black and D. M. MacRaild, *Studying History* (Basingstoke, 2007)

P. Claus and J. Marriott, *History: an Introduction to Theory, Method and Practice* (London, 2017)

A. Curthoys and A. McGrath, *How to Write the History That People Want to Read* (Basingstoke, 2011)

L. Jordanova, *History in Practice* (London, 2000)

J. Tosh with S. Lang, *The Pursuit of History: Aims, Methods and New Directions in the Study of Modern History* (London, 2006)

History of history-writing (historiography)

M. Bentley, *Modern Historiography: an Introduction* (London, 1999)

J. Black, *Clio's Battles: Historiography in Practice* (Bloomington, Ind., 2015)

P. Burke, *The French Historical Revolution: the Annales School, 1929–89* (Cambridge, 1990)

H. Chiang et al. (ed.), *Global Encyclopaedia of Lesbian, Gay, Bisexual, Transgender and Queer (LGBTQ) History* (Farmington Hills, Mich., 2019)

H. J. Kaye, *The British Marxist Historians: an Introductory Analysis* (Cambridge, 1984)

G. McLennan, *Marxism and the Methodologies of History* (London, 1981)

A. Meier and E. Rudwick, *Black History and the Historical Profession, 1915–80* (Urbana, Ill., 1986)

S. H. Rigby, *Marxism and History: a Critical Introduction* (Manchester, 1987)

H. L. Smith and M. L. Zook, *Generations of Women Historians: Within and Beyond the Academy* (Basingstoke, 2018)

J. Tendler, *Opponents of the Annales School* (Basingstoke, 2013)

D. R. Woolf, *A Concise History of History: Global Historiography from Antiquity to the Present* (Cambridge, 2019)

Theories and philosophy of history-writing (historiology)

J. M. de Bernardo Arès, *Historiology, Research and Didactics: Elaboration and Transmission of Historical Knowledge* (London, 1996)

P. J. Corfield, *Time and the Shape of History* (London, 2007)

M. Day, *The Philosophy of History: an Introduction* (London, 2008)

J. W. Moses and T. L. Knutsen (ed.), *Ways of Knowing: Competing Methodologies in Social and Political Research* (London, 2019)

A. Tucker, *Our Knowledge of the Past: a Philosophy of Historiography* (Cambridge, 2004)

Historians on studying history

M. Bloch, *The Historian's Craft*, transl. P. Putnam (Manchester, 1954, 1967)

D. Cannadine, *Making History, Now and Then: Discoveries, Controversies and Explorations* (Basingstoke, 2008)

R. G. Collingwood, *The Idea of History*, ed. T. M. Knox (pub. posthumously, 1946)

J. H. Elliott, *History in the Making* (London, 2012)

N. Ferguson (ed.), *Virtual History: Alternatives and Counterfactuals* (London, 1997; New York, 1999)

R. J. D. Munro, *Clio's Lives: Biographies and Autobiographies of Historians* (Canberra, 2017)

Historical sources (textual, including maps)

P. Carter and K. Thompson, *Sources for Local Historians* (Chichester, 2005)

M. Drake and R. Finnegan, *Sources and Methods for Family and Community Historians: a Handbook* (Cambridge, 1997)

A. Farge, *The Allure of the Archives*, transl. T. Scott-Railton (New Haven, Conn., 2013)

V. Johnson, S. Fowler and D. Thomas, *The Silence of the Archive* (London, 2017)

S. Porter, *Exploring Urban History: Sources for Local Historians* (London, 1990)

C. Steedman, *Dust* (Manchester, 2001)

Historical sources (non-textual)

C. Armstrong, *Using Non-Textual Sources: a Historian's Guide* (London, 2015)

P. Burke, *Eyewitnessing: the Uses of Images as Historical Evidence* (London, 2001)

J. Chapman, *Film and History* (Basingstoke, 2013)

L. Hannan and S. Longair, *History through Material Culture* (Manchester, 2017)

K. Harvey (ed.), *History and Material Culture: a Student's Guide to Approaching Alternative Sources* (London, 2017)

L. Jordanova, *The Look of the Past: Visual and Material Evidence in Historical Practice* (Cambridge, 2012)

R. Rosenstone, *Visions of the Past: the Challenge of Film to Our Idea of History* (Cambridge, Mass., 1995)

Useful websites

BatchGeo – <https://batchgeo.com> [accessed 30 April 2021]

Google Earth – <https://www.google.co.uk/intl/en_uk/earth> [accessed 30 April 2021]

Google Ngram Viewer – <https://books.google.com/ngrams> [accessed 30 April 2021]

The Programming Historian – <https://programminghistorian.org> [accessed 30 April 2021]

Tropy: Research Photo Management – <https://tropy.org> [accessed 30 April 2021]

Voyant – See Through Your Text – <https://voyant-tools.org> [accessed 29 April 2021]

Zotero – <https://www.zotero.org> [accessed 29 April 2021]

Historical documentation

A. Brundage, *Going to the Sources: a Guide to Historical Research and Writing* (Hoboken, N.J., 2018)

F. A. Burkle-Young and S. R. Maley, *The Art of the Footnote: the Intelligent Student's Guide to the Art and Science of Annotating Texts* (London, 1996)

A. Grafton, *The Footnote: a Curious History* (London, 1997)

Types of history

R. C. Allan, *Global Economic History: a Very Short Introduction* (London, 2019)

T. Bennett and P. Joyce (ed.), *Material Powers: Cultural Studies, History and the Material Turn* (Cham, 2010)

J. Black, *Introduction to Global Military History: 1775 to the Present Day* (London, 2018)

D. Christian, *Maps of Time: an Introduction to Big History* (London, 2004)

D. C. Coleman, *History and the Economic Past: an Account of the Rise and Decline of Economic History* (Oxford, 1987)

R. J. Evans, *Altered Pasts: Counterfactuals in History* (London, 2014)

R. Ghosh (ed.), *The Study of Social History: Recent Trends* (Kolkata, 2013)

S. Gunn, *History and Cultural Theory* (Harlow, 2006)

D. Hey, *Family Names and Family History* (London, 2000)

J. D. Hughes, *An Environmental History of the World: Humankind's Changing Role in the Community of Life* (Oxford, 2001)

S. G. Magnússon and I. M. Szijárto, *What Is Micro-History? Theory and Practice* (London, 2013)

A. Munslow (ed.), *The Routledge Companion to Historical Studies* (London, 2000)

J. Plamper, *The History of Emotions: an Introduction*, transl. K. Tribe (Oxford, 2015)

D. A. Ritchie, *Doing Oral History: a Practical Guide* (New York, 2015)

P. N. Stearns, *Gender in World History* (London, 2015)

W. Steinmetz et al. (ed.), *Writing Political History Today* (Frankfurt, 2013)

R. Wenzlhuemer, *Doing Global History: an Introduction to Six Concepts* (London, 2019)

Cliometrics (quantitative history)

A. Campbell et al., *Research Design in Social Work: Qualitative, Quantitative and Mixed Methods* (Los Angeles, Calif., 2016)

C. Feinstein and M. Thomas, *Making History Count: a Primer in Quantitative Methods for Historians* (Cambridge, 2002)

R. W. Fogel, 'The limits of quantitative methods in history', *American Historical Review*, lxxx (1975), 329–50

P. Hudson, *History by Numbers: an Introduction to Quantitative Approaches* (London, 2000)

J. S. Lyons et al. (ed.), *Reflections on the Cliometrics Revolution: Conversations with Economic Historians* (London, 2008)

Digital history (computerized big data analysis)

D. J. Cohen and R. Rosenzweig, *Digital History: a Guide to Gathering, Presenting and Preserving the Past on the Web* (Philadelphia, Pa., 2006)

A. Crymble, *Technology and the Historian: Transformations in the Digital Age* (Urbana, Ill., 2021)

L. Levenberg, T. Neilson and D. Rheams (ed.), *Research Methods for the Digital Humanities* (London, 2018)

I. Milligan, *History in the Age of Abundance: How the Web Is Transforming Historical Research* (London, 2019)

R. Risam, *New Digital Worlds: Postcolonial Digital Humanities in Theory, Practice and Pedagogy* (Evanston, Ill., 2019)

H. Salmi, *What Is Digital History?* (Cambridge, 2020)

G. Schiuma and D. Carlucci, *Big Data in the Arts and Humanities: Theory and Practice* (Boca Raton, Fla., 2018)

History, the postmodernist challenge and critical responses

P. Anderson, *The Origins of Postmodernity* (London, 1998)

C. G. Brown, *Postmodernism for Historians* (Harlow, 2005)

R. J. Evans, *In Defence of History* (London, 1997)

K. Jenkins, *Re-Thinking History* (1991, 2003)

A. Munslow, *Narrative and History* (Basingstoke, 2007)

G. Myerson, *Ecology and the End of Postmodernism* (Cambridge, 2001)

C. Norris, *What's Wrong with Postmodernism: Critical Theory and the Ends of Philosophy* (London, 1990)

N. A. Raab, *The Humanities in Transition from Postmodernism into the Digital Age* (London, 2020)

H. V. White, *The Content of Form: Narrative Discourse and Historical Representation* (London, 1973)

K. Windschuttle, *The Killing of History: How Literary Critics and Social Theorists Are Murdering Our Past* (New York, 1996)

Studying for a research degree in history

J. Felton et al., *The Professional Doctorate: a Practical Guide* (Basingstoke, 2013)

R. Murray, *How to Survive Your Viva: Defending a Thesis in an Oral Examination* (Maidenhead, 2009)

J. Wellington et al. (ed.), *Succeeding with Your Doctorate* (London, 2005)

Teaching history

W. Caferro, *Teaching History* (London, 2019)

J. Cannon, *Teaching History at University* (London, 1984)

A. Flint and S. Jack, *Approaches to Learning and Teaching History: a Toolkit for International Teachers* (Cambridge, 2018)

T. M. Kelly, *Teaching History in the Digital Age* (Ann Arbor, Mich., 2013)

R. B. Simon et al. (ed.), *Teaching Big History* (Oakland, Calif., 2015)

Historians and public history

D. Armitage and J. Guldi, *The History Manifesto* (Cambridge, 2014)

S. Berger (ed.), *Perspectives on the Intersection between Politics, Activism and the Historical Profession* (New York, 2019)

J. de Groot, *Consuming History: Historians and Heritage in Contemporary Popular Culture* (London, 2016)

M. Finn and K. Smith (ed.), *New Paths to Public Histories* (Basingstoke, 2015)

J. B. Gardner and P. Hamilton (ed.), *The Oxford Handbook of Public History* (New York, 2017)

J. L. Koslow, *Public History: an Introduction from Theory to Application* (London, 2021)

J. Wojdon and D. Wisniewska (ed.), *Public in Public History* (London, 2021)

Index

Index